ABOUT THE AUTHOR

Sarah Rossbach is an author and feng shui consultant who lives with her family in New Jersey, USA. Whilst living and working in Hong Kong she learned the art of feng shui from the worldwide authority Professor Lin Yun. She has written articles on the subject for *The New York Times*, *House & Garden* and *Harper's Bazaar*.

By the same author

Feng Shui (Rider)

Sarah Rossbach

INTERIOR DESIGN WITH

Feng Shui

Foreword and Calligraphy by Professor Lin Yun

FENG SHUI CONCEPTS

RIDER
LONDON SYDNEY AUCKLAND JOHANNESBURG

3 5 7 9 10 8 6 4

Published by Rider,
an imprint of Ebury Press, Random House,
20 Vauxhall Bridge Road, London SW1V 2SA
www.randomhouse.co.uk

Random House Australia (Pty) Limited
20 Alfred Street, Milsons Point, Sydney,
New South Wales 2061, Australia

Random House New Zealand Limited
18 Poland Road, Glenfield
Auckland 10, New Zealand

Random House South Africa (Pty) Limited
Endulini, 5A Jubilee Road,
Parktown 2193, South Africa
www.randomhouse.co.uk

The Random House Group Limited Reg. No. 954009

First published in the UK in 1987 by Rider Books
Reprinted 1990
New edition 1991
Reprinted 1991, 1993, 1994, 1995 (twice), 1996, 1997
This edition published in 1999.

Calligraphy by Lin Yun

Papers used by Rider Books are natural, recyclable products
made from wood grown in sustainable forests.

Printed and bound in Great Britain by
Cox and Wyman, Reading, Berks.

A CIP catalogue record for this book
is available from the British Library

ISBN 0-7126-7002-5

To Lin Yun
Who taught me more than I know

CONTENTS

Photo gallery follows page 100.

FOREWORD

BUDDHA

There are many ways to understand life and the universe: through superstition, religion, philosophy, science, and so forth. While each approach has its own experts—scientists, priests, philosophers, doctors, poets—all are merely blind men receiving different impressions from touching the same elephant. A priest may feel its legs and say life is like a tree trunk; a scientist holding its tail may find that life is ropelike; a poet feeling an ear may proclaim life like a lotus leaf; a doctor holding its tusk may conclude that life is like a bone; a philosopher grasping its trunk may pronounce life to be like a snake; and so on. From his own perspective, each expert's conclusion is knowledgeable and makes sense. Their theories, however, are merely parts of the whole picture.

I, too, am one of the blind. And because I touch a different part of the elephant, I have developed my own theory about the relationship of the universe to human life. My insights come from China—a vast and varied country roughly the size of the United States—which, during its five thousand years of civilization, has spawned many diverse and deep concepts. Among the most arcane yet practical of these concepts is *feng shui*.

According to feng shui, our life and destiny are closely interwoven with the workings of the universe and nature. All permutations, from cosmic to atomic, resonate within us. The force that links man and his surroundings is called *ch'i* (translated as human spirit, energy, or cosmic breath). There are different kinds of ch'i: a kind that circulates in the earth, a kind that circulates in the atmosphere, and a kind that moves within our own bodies. Each of us possesses ch'i. Ch'i carries our bodies. Yet its characteristics and the ways in which it moves us are different in each of us. Ch'i is the breath essential to maintaining physical, environmental, and emotional balance. The point of feng shui is to harness and enhance environmental ch'i to improve the flow of ch'i within our bodies, thus improving our life and destiny.

Harmony and balance are both crucial factors in feng shui—they pervade the *process* linking man and the universe. And that process is called *Tao*.

The Chinese link man to heaven and earth through Tao, dividing all things into complementary dualities—*yin* and *yang*. Tao is a thread linking humans with their surroundings—be it a dwelling or an office, a mountain or a river, the earth or even the cosmos. Tao works this way: Look at the sky—is it empty, or is it full of atmosphere, sun, moon, and stars? Maybe it is, maybe it isn't. Out of the sky comes heaven (yang) and earth (yin), within earth exist mountains and plains (yin), and rivers and streams (yang). On the mountains and plains, people (yang) live and build houses (yin). There are males (yang) and females (yin), and each has an exterior (yang) and an interior (yin).

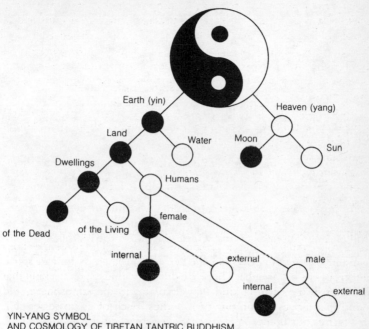

YIN-YANG SYMBOL
AND COSMOLOGY OF TIBETAN TANTRIC BUDDHISM

Out of the interaction—balancing and harmonizing—of the forces of yin and yang arises the theory of ch'i—meaning both cosmic breath and human energy or spirit. Ch'i is the most essential feature of life. Human ch'i determines our movements, physical characteristics, and personal traits.

When I talk about why humans can move, I completely accept biological explanations about the process of the brain signaling muscles to move our joints and bones. In addition, however, I see man as a breath of ch'i. Because of ch'i, we can move. Ch'i animates the mouth so that we can speak. It flows through the legs so that we can walk. It circulates in the hands so that we can write. If it only fills part of our body, however, we will be partially paralyzed.

The way ch'i carries and fills our bodies indicates our health and destiny, not to mention how we interact in society, how we affect others and our immediate surroundings, and—in the case of world leaders—how we affect the world. Therefore, one's ch'i influences the self, others, society, and the universe.

Ch'i is the nonbiological self—our spirit, our psyche, our essence. Without ch'i, a body is merely a corpse of skin, bones, and muscle. Within two or three years, our cells regenerate. Our bodies are continually changing, yet our *self* is basically the same—and the constant factor is ch'i.

Ch'i is the essence that makes a six-year-old child we have not seen for three years recognizable to us. Although all the child's cells have died and been replaced with new ones, there is a quality that remains distinctive and distinguishable. And that quality is ch'i. Ch'i is our destiny and also *creates* it.

To improve human ch'i and destiny, feng shui offers many theories, therapies, and techniques that I have developed and refined in my practice.

In my teaching, ch'i develops from airborne particles of embryonic ch'i called *ling,* which circulate in the atmosphere. The universe is full of different kinds of ling. Once ling enters the mother's womb, it becomes our self, our spirit, and our ch'i. It fills and carries our bodies. Once the person is born, ch'i will help him develop and fulfill his destiny. In old age, when ch'i departs from the body, the person will die and ch'i will become ling again (see Appendix 2).

During our lives, our ch'i is affected by many things: the self, others, fashion, the environment. Ch'i is the wind carrying the seeds of change, customs, and trends, on a global or a personal level; for example, the effects of dollar fluctuations or the defaulting of a devel-

LING

oping nation's loan on the worldwide economic situation, or merely the contagious nature of panic, sickness, or laughter. For instance, if a country is taken over by a coup d'état, neighboring nations may also suffer unrest or even the same fate. If a fellow plane passenger gets airsick, you may feel nauseous too. Fall fashions in Paris may influence New York styles in winter and California styles in spring. The medium that purveys these trends and feelings is ch'i.

Home ch'i can also affect our personal ch'i. The study of the influence of environmental ch'i on personal ch'i is an important part of feng shui. For instance, if your entrance door opens onto a wall, then your ch'i will be blocked. Having to move around the wall as soon as you enter will affect your posture, and coming up against the wall will make you feel defeated, lowering your expectations in life. As a result, you will struggle. Also, for example, the bed should be the most comfortable place to lie down and relax. If the bed is next to a door that creaks when you sleep, watch TV, or read, you will feel a presence as though someone is entering. Naturally you will accumulate a sensitivity, and the cumulative experience will affect your mental stability; your heart will beat faster, you will be more excitable. Thus, there will be a great impact on the balance of the nervous system with similar consequences. If you work with your back to the door, you will partially expect someone to enter behind you and interrupt you. As a result, your effectiveness and productivity will decrease. This will psychologically hurt you.

Therefore, Black Hat sect feng shui (see glossary) perceives life as more than a hermetically sealed entity. To explain our life course, linear thinking is not enough. Greater depth—a combination of planes of thought—is needed to decipher the events of our life. A multitude of factors and dimensions affect our ch'i and our life. If something happens, there are many reasons for it. To discern these reasons, I use both vertical and horizontal analysis.

Vertical analysis links our lives to our immediate and cosmic, or larger, environments. It must consider the universe and the movement and positions of stars, sun, and moon, as well as weather patterns, tides, and atmospheric conditions. Nor can it overlook the political, geographic, and economic situations of our nation, from the mores and customs of our society to our state, city, neighborhood, yard, house, bedroom, bed, and finally ourselves. All these factors affect our ch'i. But the closer the environmental factor is, the greater the influence it possesses.

Other factors can be understood from horizontal analysis, which examines the relationship of peripheral elements to causality and probability.

A person doesn't merely die, get married, or lose a job. There are many possible and seemingly unrelated factors and occurrences leading to such an event. For instance, why did a certain woman die? Immediate reasons tell us she was old and sick. But horizontal analysis links her death to other factors, such as a broken vase. She may have tipped over an expensive vase belonging to her daughter-in-law, who, in turn, scolded her. In a fit of self-anger, she rushes out into the cold without a coat and walks to her friend's house to play mah-jongg. There, still upset, she loses, making her mood worse. So she leaves in a huff, refusing a jacket even though it is now raining. She catches cold and subsequently dies. Thus her death can be traced back to the vase or even further.

Closely linked to these multiple factors affecting our life is destiny. Some people say life is predetermined by karma (good deeds), the stars, and so on. Some don't believe in destiny at all. Others believe primarily in their own will and ability to create their lives. I believe that we each have a destiny that can be altered, not just by our own rational efforts or karma, but by mystical means that seem to defy logic.

Through our own will and self-cultivation, our lives can follow a desired path, although unforeseen events can change its course. It is similar to cultivating a melon. A melon seed, with the help of sun, fertile soil, rain, and a farmer's effort, should grow into a melon. But in fact, even under the best of conditions, this is not a sure thing; anything can happen. For example, through careful cultivation, the seed will grow into a fat and juicy melon. But the morning it is to be harvested, a child may step on it.

The feng shui introduced in this book tells us how to use its cures to change our destiny for the better.

When you buy a house, there are some basic rules to follow. Black Hat sect feng shui operates on two levels, *sying* and *yi.*

Sying encompasses the tangible environmental factors of feng shui: it denotes the external elements—energy (ch'i) of land, shape and structure of houses and columns, juxtaposition of doors, furniture placement—that contribute to the feng shui of a place to determine one's luck. Traditional feng shui schools mostly emphasize sying—literally "shapes"—and directions.

While not rejecting these traditional methods, the Black Hat sect includes an additional instrument to harmonize the environment: the channeling and balancing of ch'i. My theory, besides embracing sying, also includes something extra: yi. Yi—loosely translated as a wish, a will, or an intention—plays an important role in Black Hat sect feng shui. Yi is a blessing, a way of adjusting and enhancing ch'i through intuition and imposition of the will of the expert (and the will to believe of the client) on a house or a person. It is a vital but intangible process—a positive transference and transformation of energy (ch'i)—that reinforces and blesses the physical aspect (sying) of feng shui.

Here is how these two categories can be further broken down:

SYING
1. earth ch'1
2. earth shapes
3. building shapes
4. room arrangement
5. others

Internal Factors
1. stove position
2. beams
3. stairs
4. columns
5. doors
6. desk-study

7. dining table
8. desk-office
9. wall or furniture colors
10. lights
11. others

External Factors
1. road direction
2. bridges
3. trees
4. roof top
5. corners
6. temple or shrine in front or back of house
7. rivers and streams
8. telephone or electricity poles
9. colors of surroundings
10. others

YI
1. Three Secrets
2. ba-gua
3. Tracing the Nine Stars
4. Eight-Door Wheel
5. Yu-nei (adjusting house ch'i—internal)

6 Yu-wai (adjusting house ch'i—external)
7. Constantly Turning Dharma Wheel
8. house history
9. others

(If you ask me what aspect in each category is most important, I will tell you "others": the subtle signs that identify and shape our destiny.)

I use both sying and yi to analyze and then to improve a given area's feng shui. Sying, which is easier to grasp and enact, is explained in the earlier sections of this book. The rules of sying tell you how physical surroundings are affecting you and how, by adjusting and altering them, you can change specific aspects of your life, if not your destiny. For example, sying may refer to a poorly placed bed that brings chronic colds and a multitude of taxing problems; two unaligned doors that create family discord; or a tree near the entrance that blocks career development. Sying also refers to the physical ways to improve an area's feng shui.

Yi, on the other hand, requires much more study. Yi is the use of our mental powers to cultivate the ch'i of a house or a person. Besides being highly intuitive, yi is a complex and detailed aspect of feng shui. This element must be learned orally from a master and needs years of training to perfect. It is introduced later in the book for readers wishing a deeper understanding of feng shui.

There are many schools of feng shui, and my discipline—the Black Hat sect of Tibetan Tantric Buddhism (TTB)—occupies an important place among feng shui schools. I first encountered the Black Hat sect more than forty-five years ago, in Peking. When I was six or seven years old, I would often play with friends on the grounds of a local lamasery, a monastery in Peking of Tibetan Buddhist lamas. There, one day, a high lama—a Buddhist scholar and an expert in the Black Hat sect's mystical arts—took me under his wing. For ten years he taught me Black Hat sect mystical methods, including feng shui theory and practice. Later I apprenticed with other well-known masters and acquired feng shui experience.

I find that the Black Hat sect's teachings are the most useful, up-to-date, and compatible with modern science and design. Yet they also rely on ancient Chinese Taoist culture and thought—Tao, yin-yang, ch'i, and traditional feng shui—not to mention influences from Indian and Tibetan Buddhist beliefs and practices.

My method of Black Hat sect feng shui is an outgrowth of various religious disciplines. Black Hat sect feng shui evolved out of the long journey of Buddhism from India through Tibet and into China. In each place it absorbed indigenous teachings: From India it brought an organized church complete with yoga, chants, compassion, and dharma, and the sacred discipline of transmitting teaching from master to pupil. In Tibet it incorporated the mystical chants and charms of Bon, the native religion. And in China proper it absorbed the *I Ching* and Confucian, Taoist, and folk religions and customs such as traditional feng shui, palmistry, face reading, faith healing, and the theory of ch'i. The synthesis is a very practical and sensitive approach to surroundings, suffused and supported by a repertoire of mystical chants and charms, prayers, and meditation. These religious influences give Black Hat sect feng shui extra clout, producing far more successful results than those produced by other schools!

In its journey to the West, Black Hat sect feng shui today has also absorbed new customs and inventions. Its cures include lights, electricity, and heavy machinery. Rum has replaced the strong rice wine used in ritual concoctions. And placement of microwave ovens and computers is given serious thought. But despite modernization, the aim of feng shui remains the same as it was thousands of years ago: the pursuit and creation of a more comfortable and harmonious place to live and work.

Traditionally, the mystical knowledge and practice of Black Hat sect feng shui has been orally transmitted from master to pupil and has never been written down. I have designated Sarah Rossbach, a writer and former language student of mine, to be the first ever to write a volume totally devoted to Black Hat sect feng shui. She has directly received all information from me, and I feel she has grasped and explained my theories, teachings, and practices with lucidity. I am not only pleased to introduce this unique and important book, but I am also grateful to Sarah for translating both my teachings and this introduction.

—Lin Yun

PREFACE

This book is written as a how-to manual. It seeks to teach the practical applications of feng shui. Yet it is not a how-to design book in the strict sense. People looking for ways to make a "design statement" or for hard-and-fast feng shui rules for every possible occasion may well be disappointed. Taste and style remain the realm of the reader. The value of the book increases with the amount of intuition, intelligence, and inventiveness that the reader brings to it. This book acts as a guide to spatial arrangements, offering concepts, examples, and methods of achieving harmony with one's environment. It offers many rules and resolutions, but these are only suggestions to enable readers to educate themselves in order to interpret their homes in ways suitable to their individual needs and preferences.

Feng shui encompasses a dimension of interior design that can enhance and complement any style. Some established Western interior designers and architects have consulted feng shui experts for both professional and personal purposes.

The book contains hundreds of examples of design problems and cures, but the reader will find few calculations—and no doubt many shapes, permutations, and arrangements are missing. But that is not the point. Once you understand the principles explained in these pages, you can apply them to many situations. For example, once you grasp the concept that a position at the end of a long corridor can be inauspicious, creating health and career problems because energy is channeled down a corridor too swiftly, you can apply this to other situations. You will thus know that you should avoid straight, arrow-like rivers and roads aiming at a site, and should beware of the "funnel" effect of three or more doors or windows in a row, which also conduct energy too quickly.

Using the guidelines in this book, you should weigh the impact of each situation. Judgment is an important component of feng shui: the road that seems to aim at your house might be a much-traveled expressway that shoots energy and traffic dangerously toward your home, or it may only be a tiny lane leading to a sleepy cul-de-sac having little adverse effect on your life.

Similarly, many cures are interchangeable, and there is leeway for individual taste and ingenuity. For example, if you have a corner jutting threateningly into your bedroom, and the suggested cures are inappropriate for your taste (you hate mirrors and have no luck with plants), you could obscure the corner's malign impact by hanging something of your choice, such as a silk bell-pull and tassel similar to those hung in old European villas and hotels.

The impact of feng shui is wide-ranging and offers a unique way of dealing with problems in our living space or personal lives.

I offer, however, one caveat. Having the best feng shui may not always prevent the inevitable—the death of grandparents or parents, jealousy at work, or day-to-day hassles. It will, though, position you to cope better or rebound faster. A New York caterer comments that after she placed a mirror behind her stove and a bell at the entrance to the kitchen, "My reactions changed; when a wedding cake was giving me trouble, instead of getting frustrated and throwing in the towel, I patiently continued working on it and eventually it came together beautifully."

When Professor Lin advises people, he always offers a two-part answer to their problems: the cure and the principles behind the cure. Many people are only interested in the cure and are happy to learn nothing more. Those who absorb the theories may be able to help themselves the next time.

ACKNOWLEDGMENTS

Researching and writing this book was not a simple task. Many people contributed time, information, and suggestions that not only made this book possible, but also greatly enriched it.

I would like to thank the following people for their kind and generous help and encouragement: Vivian and Wilson Chang, Professor and Mrs. Leo Ch'en, Jenny Cheung, Bill Doyle, Deborah Herron, Al Holm, Margaret Huang, Johnny and Lola Kao, David Keh, Sally Keil, William Robert King & Associates, Architects, Michelle and Gordon Jin, Thomas Lee, Rosina Lee, Sue Lehmann, Mr. T. C. Liang, Virginia Liu, Mr. and Mrs. George Lu, Howard Rossbach, Eleanor Rossbach, Maureen St. Onge, Ed Schoenfeld, Professor S. Y. Shieh, Patrick Smith, Ann Sperry, Edgar Sung, Charles Wang, Robert Wang, Elke Ward-Smith, Alice Wong, Ken Yeh, Richard Zak, the Lin Yun Foundation, and the Chinese Cultural and Philosophical Foundation.

I would like to thank Betsy Scanlon and Dorothy Harrington for their noble efforts in decoding my handwriting. I am grateful to Betty Ann Crawford, Rachelle Epstein, Douglas Fleming, Spencer Reiss, and Tim Smith for their valuable comments, and to Glenn Cowley and Caroline Press for their editorial encouragement, insights, and suggestions.

I am especially grateful to Jon Zatkin, Lynn Tu, Lily Hwoo, and Chu Chien-lih for aiding my research, making information available and intelligible to me, and responding to my calls for help.

For the photographs in this book I would like to thank Dudley Gray for patiently and artistically pursuing the desired results. I also gratefully acknowledge Andrzej Janerka and Norman McGrath, who each supplied a photograph. For their help in providing sites for the photographs I would like to thank the following: Wilson and Vivian Chang, Clodagh, Douglas Fleming, Fred Gluck, Patty Hambrecht of K.B.H. Interiors Inc, David Keh, Sally Keil, Sue Lehmann, Sean McCarthy, I.M. Pei and Partners, and Ann Sperry.

Above all, my thanks go to Professor Lin for his patient instruction, valuable advice, and warm friendship during all stages of this project, and—most important—without whom this book would never have been. . . .

GLOSSARY

ba-gua The eight trigrams of the *I Ching,* to which are ascribed eight
characteristics relating to nature, man, family relationships, and
even areas within a home. It is also the octagonal symbol of the
I Ching. The octagon can be superimposed on a home, a plot of
land, an office, a room, or even furniture to diagnose environmental ills affecting residents. It also can be used to cure these
problems.

Black Hat Sect An unorthodox sect of Tibetan Tantric Buddhism
that in China mixed Tibetan Buddhism and Tibetan Bon with
indigenous Chinese beliefs and practices. It combines religious
and philosophical Taoism, Confucianism, folk cures and customs,
and feng shui.

ch'i Cosmic breath or energy ascribed to the atmosphere, the earth,
and humans. This is the most important principle that feng shui
experts seek to alter; they channel and enhance environmental
ch'i flow to improve human ch'i and thus increase happiness,
wealth, and vitality.

chu-shr The yet-to-be-discovered; that which is outside science and
our range of knowledge; "illogical" cures.

feng shui Literally translated as "wind and water," it is the Chinese
art of placement, of balancing and enhancing the environment.

I Ching An early mystical text of divination—the mother of Chinese thought—used to tell fortunes and to give guidance. Its texts offer wisdom and depict the universe and man's fate in constant flux. Its trigrams embody an early cosmology linking nature and man, and provide a mystical chart where human fate is directly linked to surroundings.

ju-sha Powdered cinnabar (red mercuric sulfide) used as a mystical medicine in feng shui cures and rituals. Ju-sha is poisonous so care should be taken when using it.

ling Tiny airborne particles of embryonic ch'i—the prenatal and post-death spirit of an individual.

mantra A ritualistic chant that, combined with a mudra and a wish, blesses a home or an individual to enhance environmental and human ch'i.

mudra A hand blessing—often similar to hand gestures of the Buddha—which, with a mantra and a wish, can bless or exorcise a place or a person.

ru-shr That which is known, within our scope of experience and knowledge; "logical" cures.

sying Forms, the immanent aspect of feng shui—what we can see, feel, and move, ranging from earth shapes, landscaping, road directions, houses, and rooms to furniture placement.

syong huang Powdered realgar—a red-orangish mineral consisting of arsenic sulfide—sometimes interchangeable with ju-sha, but also having its own specific uses in mystical cures. Syong huang is poisonous, so care should be taken when using it.

Tao "The Way," a philosophical concept of unity of opposites that describes the true nature and harmonious governing principles of man and the universe.

Taoism Both a philosophy and a religion. As a philosophy, it preaches transcendence of the mundane through identifying with Tao and the laws of nature; as a popular religion, it integrates Chinese custom and wisdom, encompassing folklore, astrology, herbal medicine, and feng shui to help devotees achieve worldly success, happiness, and comfort.

TTB Tibetan Tantric Buddhism—a form of Buddhism prevailing in Tibet derived from Indian Mahayana Buddhism. Based on the esoteric mysticism of Tantra (tradition of ritual and yoga) and on Bon (a primitive and mystic religion of Tibet). See Black Hat sect.

yi Intentions or wishes; the intuitive, transcendental part of feng shui. It incorporates blessings, meditations, and ritual practices both to strengthen the practical, sying cures and to adjust and alter ch'i from negative to positive.

yin-and-yang theory The Taoist concept that unites all opposites.

INTERIOR DESIGN WITH
Feng Shui

1

INTRODUCTION

These characters, k'an yü, mean "cover" and "support." Loosely translated as "under the canopy of heaven," this was the ancient term for feng shui.

Until recent years, the wisdom of feng shui has been the domain of a handful of sinologists, some Buddhist and Taoist priests, and a sprinkling of experts—feng shui professors—who, on a professional basis, advise clients on anything from where to buy a house to siting an ancestor's grave*. A household word in many parts of Asia, feng shui is a cross between an art and a science. Its goal is to arrange buildings, rooms, and furniture in the most beneficial way to achieve maximum harmony with nature. According to Chinese beliefs, once this is achieved, prosperity and happiness will follow. Traditionally, the knowledge is passed down from father to son, who dispense information only after a fee is presented in a red "lucky money" envelope. Yet, while most Chinese know some basic rules—both helpful and superstitious—few have an opportunity to master feng shui. Instead, when moving into a home or an office, they consult books or seek out guidance from feng shui professors, who practice feng shui according to varying methods and levels of expertise.

This is my second book on feng shui. My first book, *Feng Shui: The Chinese Art of Placement,* published by E. P. Dutton in 1983, gave a theoretical and historical background of this millennia-old practice. It was necessarily quite academic. In my early research of feng shui in Hong Kong and New York, my personal experience began with applying it to my own home and those of my friends. Chiefly, I was an interested observer, but those days were soon to end.

Shortly after the book was published, I was deluged with requests to act as a professional feng shui consultant on how to create more comfortable, if not luckier, homes and offices. My first experience was a New York artist's loft. I wandered through the studio-home and began to apply textbook rules of feng shui: steep stairs leading down from the entrance funneled money and opportunity out the door; the entrance opened into the dining area, so guests came more to eat and less to appreciate the artist's talent; an awkwardly placed bed brought nagging health woes and a stream of annoying problems. The artist was impressed—and I was amazed—that these and other observations were true. After installing a screen to shield the kitchen from the entrance, she found her guests paying more attention to her work and less to their stomachs.

A number of similar experiences taught me that examining a place's feng shui was similar to reading a palm. By inspecting the layout of furniture and the structural formations in a room, an astute and intuitive observer could tell the patterns of a person's life:

---

*This book covers only the homes of the living. See *Feng Shui: The Chinese Art of Placement* for grave-siting information.

- an office desk where each successive occupant got demoted
- a door alignment that created a division between two business partners
- a poorly sited kitchen that encouraged binge eating

As a result of the past three years of feng shui consulting, I have gained a greater understanding, knowledge, and awareness of the workings of feng shui. I realized that, although my first book provided a clear introduction to feng shui, more graphic and detailed information was needed. The additional instruction will enable those wishing to apply feng shui to their own lives to do so with a fuller appreciation of this art. As with the first book, this endeavor would not have been possible without the guidance of one man, Dr. Lin Yun, a leading feng shui expert and an educator in the field of Chinese culture and philosophy—specifically the Black Hat sect of feng shui. The Black Hat sect of Tibetan Tantric Buddhism is a mixture of Indian Buddhism and Bon, an indigenous Tibetan religion that combines animism, mysticism, and folk rituals.

I stumbled upon feng shui in 1977 while studying Chinese with Professor Lin Yun in Hong Kong. He was a friendly and portly man with a sartorial bent toward Hawaiian shirts, black slacks, and slightly elevated shoes. Rumors flew in the British colony of his prowess in an ancient, mystical art called feng shui. I had heard of this practice, but had only a vague idea of what it was. Soon, however, I had an opportunity to learn more, because our classes were regularly disrupted by the frantic appearance of a desperate believer who had tracked down Lin Yun and would not leave until his latest problem —a rocky marriage, a failing business, poor health—was attended to. So, as if on cue, we'd close our textbook and Lin Yun would invite me to join him on what might be called feng shui field trips.

I soon learned that this age-old science was at once both mystical and pragmatic. It has ancient origins dating back thousands of years to the beginning of Chinese civilization, but is used today for the most sophisticated of purposes.

Feng shui is an important piece in an intricate and intriguing Chinese puzzle of life and the universe. It influences—and is influenced by—everything from landscape and urban design to landscape painting and poetry, alchemy and astrology, and even ancient forms of philosophy, science, and psychology.

Translated as "wind" and "water," feng shui is an "eco-art" linking man and his destiny with his surroundings, be they natural or man-made, cosmic or local. For thousands of years the Chinese have sought to channel, harness, and harmonize environmental forces, such as wind and water, to improve the landscape and, ultimately, their lives. They have believed that if they were ideally positioned within the universe, they could enhance the balance of nature and thus improve their fortunes; for them, poor feng shui portended imbalance and disaster.

A product of early Chinese thought, feng shui evolved as a mix of Taoism, Buddhism, the yin-yang theory of balance and oneness with nature, common sense, superstition, and, sometimes, good taste. While feng shui tools range from furniture and building placement to the I Ching, they are reinforced by the expert's intuition, imagination, and interpretation of the environment. Its longevity can be ascribed to its promise of bestowing good things: happy marriage, family, long life, wealth, and a successful career.

Today, those in powerful positions do not take chances where feng shui is involved. I was surprised to find hard-nosed businessmen anxious to try feng shui as an added tool to clinch deals, enhance corporate clout, or expand their businesses. Modern-day home builders, decorators, restaurateurs, and such mighty international corporations as the Chase Manhattan Bank, Citibank, and Morgan Guaranty Trust in Hong Kong, Singapore, and Taiwan are not above calling on experts in this science for help. Singapore's Cambridge-educated prime minister, Lee Kuan-yu, held monthly consultations with a feng shui expert, but tragedies befell him politically and personally when he ignored the advice to stop filling in the city-state's shoreline, thereby unbalancing the country's feng shui. Indeed, the purpose of feng shui practices is to deflect ill fortune and attract good luck.

While researching this book, I again sought out Lin Yun, who had relocated to California. He was lecturing three times a week on feng shui and related Chinese arts.

Now sporting Chinese silk mandarin jackets, he was often surrounded by admirers, mostly expatriates from Taiwan, ranging from scholars to businesspeople. When he was not teaching or advising on the layout of a bank or a restaurant, he seemed to be on a continual lecture circuit—the United Nations, Stanford, Berkeley, San Francisco State, Yale, Harvard, MIT, and Cornell universities, and the University of Iowa, to name a few—explaining, in mandarin Chinese, sometimes with the help of a translator, the workings of feng shui.

I flew out to California, where—between consultations at a Chinese restaurant and a video store—he began to introduce me to a more sacred, mystical side of the art. This mysticism has been inherent in feng shui for centuries and seems to add strength to the practical aspects of its cures. Although some cures seem logical, I am still not sure why feng shui works—why a few simple, seemingly inconsequential alterations in the environment can make it more comfortable, more positively imbued; perhaps the answer is beyond our current level of knowledge.

The body of this book will provide the more functional rules and methods—give or take a little mysticism. The final chapter and the appendices offer more technical and mystical information for those wishing to go beyond the basics.

Feng shui without mysticism is like a body without a soul. Those seeking a deeper view of feng shui will find in the appendices a sampling of Dr. Lin's more advanced teachings, the profounder aspects of the Black Hat sect of Tibetan Tantric Buddhism. On their own, they are a bit of an academic exercise, because traditionally their power comes from being orally transmitted, once the expert has received a red envelope with money in it.

All instruction in this book is taken from Lin Yun's teachings. I have not edited out information that might not appeal to Western tastes. Indeed, many chants, rituals, and traditional cures that may put off some readers are acceptable in modern Eastern lives. They are personal blessings and techniques often practiced in solitude to set in motion a positive mental process. Whether one calls it hocus-pocus, the will to believe, or the power of positive thinking, the function of rituals is to increase our receptivity so we can reap the maximum benefits from the process.

The feng shui taught by Lin Yun addresses the way we deal with our immediate environment—how it shapes our lives. As I followed him on his rounds, this all made a great deal of sense. Most of us have had a sense of dread on entering one place, or have felt happy in another. Feng shui attempts to define what elements in our environment depress and elevate us. It also identifies design problems and offers simple "cures" to balance and enhance our surroundings and —with luck—our lives.

2

BASIC CONCEPTS

FENG SHUI PERSPECTIVE

Chinese palaces of antiquity and modern multinational corporate headquarters in Asia share a guiding principle for the siting and design of their buildings—feng shui, the Chinese art of placement. The premise of feng shui has remained the same—the pursuit of the most harmonious and auspicious place to live and to work. For thousands of years the Chinese have felt that their lives were magically linked to their environment. They believed that certain places were better, luckier, and more sacred than others, and that features of the environment—hills, streams, roads, walls, and doors—all could affect a person. They concluded that if a person changed and balanced his surroundings, he could balance and improve his life. As Lin Yun explains, "I adapt homes and offices to harmonize with the currents of ch'i," meaning man's energy and cosmic breath. "The shapes of beds, the forms and heights of buildings, the directions of roads and corners all modify a person's destiny."

Though records of feng shui go back to the fourth century B.C., its concepts and practice most likely began centuries—if not millennia—earlier, as Chinese farmers first settled along the Wei and Yellow river valleys. Human survival and successful cultivation of crops were primary concerns. Both depended on the caprice and cycles of heaven and earth—rain, flood, sun, frost, drought. The Chinese saw their fate as inextricably entwined with the creative and destructive powers of vast and awesome nature, and their fortunes bound to the mysterious workings of the entire universe. The early Chinese people sought harmony with the force of nature. Heaven and earth were perceived as animistic powers—often dragons—that inhaled and exhaled ch'i, a life-enhancing energy.

The landscape was venerated. China's religions, philosophies, poetry, and landscape scrolls often reflected a desire to capture and identify with the power and beauty, balance and immortality of nature. To go against nature's course, the Chinese believed, would ultimately hurt man. So, when building a city, a road, or a farm, they took great pains to avoid disturbing the earth's flesh. To survive, prosper, and avoid injuring an earthly dragon, the Chinese called on shamans, who, like architectural dowsers, searched out ch'i to discern the optimal place to build a farm, a temple, or a house, or to site an entire city or an ancestor's grave.

Today, mastering feng shui requires many years of training—as well as an intuitive talent. During the training, ancient Chinese philosophy and religion are incorporated. This book describes the elementary procedures of the practice. Before doing so, however, it is necessary to mention the conceptual pillars of feng shui. The more you understand them, the easier it will be to grasp the rules and the working procedures of feng shui. Let's look at *Tao* (pronounced "dow").

TAO

TAO AND YIN-YANG

Tao is a process and a principle linking man with the universe. The Chinese have a saying: "Everything in accordance with Tao." Translated as "way" or "path," Tao reflects the natural way, the eternal rhythm of the universe and the way of man within it. The concept of Tao evolved out of ancient Chinese observations of nature and identification with it. They saw that nature was constantly in flux yet cyclical, and that their crops and fates were determined by and depended on the way of nature. Man and nature follow the same laws. As a *principle,* Tao is a wholeness stemming from balance, a harmonious union of interacting opposites. As a *process,* Tao is constant, cyclical change, opposites spawning each other—the yearly cycle of summer leading to winter, returning to summer. Through understanding the patterns of Tao, feng shui experts seek balance and equilibrium to achieve harmony with the environment.

Out of Tao came *yin* and *yang,* the two primordial forces that govern the universe. They are complementary opposites, and together they make up all aspects of life and matter. Yin is dark, yang is light; yin is passive, yang is active. When united, however, they are harmony—Tao. They depend on each other—without cold, the concept *hot* does not exist, without new there is no old, without life there is no death.

Yin also exists within yang, and yang exists within yin.

YIN AND YANG

The Chinese link heaven, earth, and man through Tao, dividing all things into complementary dualities. The yin-yang concept links humans with their surroundings—be they a dwelling or an office, a mountain or a river, the earth or even the cosmos. Master the connections, as feng shui teaches, and you can maintain inner balance and improve your fortunes and destiny.

For example, in homes and offices, a balance of yin and yang is desirable. The influence of Tao and yin and yang come into play in nearly all aspects of design. Feng shui seeks to find and create a balanced and harmonious home, and thus to bring the occupants both good health and emotional equilibrium. This idea of balance is more sophisticated than mere symmetry. It aligns a home or a person with the natural and man-made elements, thus creating a peaceful, harmonious flow within the environment. For instance, a house facing a pond—in line with the natural elements—will have a more positive effect than one merely sited in the middle of a square suburban plot. However, if that pond (yang) is so large it overpowers the house (yin), a balancing rock or garden must be installed to harmonize these elements. Tao also comes into play when resolving an awkwardly shaped house or room. In this case, another feature—a light, a plant, or an interior mirror—can be used to restore architectural balance.

CH'I

According to Professor Lin, there are many influences that affect our life course: luck, feng shui, destiny, good acts that create good karma, as well as diligence, study, and self-cultivation. But the most important consideration is ch'i (pronounced "chee"). Indeed, ch'i—translated as "breath" or "energy"—is the most important concept in feng shui.

Ch'i is a unifying principle of energy linking everything from the powerful blow of a kung-fu expert or the brushstroke of a calligrapher to the flow of water or the shape of a hill.

Ch'i is the leading factor affecting human life. Translated as "breath," ch'i is an energy or force that creates mountains and volcanoes, directs streams and rivers, and determines the colors and shapes of trees and plants. This energy is also known as "dragon points," which are similar to the energy paths that ancient Druids traced in Europe. In feng shui, experts prospect for veins of good or "nourishing" ch'i and then channel and refine it to enrich the lives and ch'i of residents.

CH'I

In humans, ch'i is the spirit or vital force that carries the body—the way we appear and act, and how we move and talk. Our movements are governed by the glow of ch'i and the way we direct it through our bodies. If ch'i cannot circulate in our legs, we will be paralyzed. If it cannot flow to our hands, we will not be able to move our fingers. If it cannot reach the heart, death will ensue.

Ch'i is with us from birth to death. To the Chinese, conception is not simply the union of sperm and egg. It also involves an embryonic form of ch'i called *ling*. Ling are tiny airborne particles (or molecular charges) that circulate in the universe and enter the womb at conception. When a baby is born, its ling becomes its ch'i. When we die, our ch'i joins the limitless pool of ling.

Ch'i is different in each person. It moves us. It can flow up or down. Ch'i determines whether we stand straight, slouch, or limp.

The ideal is to have balanced ch'i that flows smoothly throughout the body. It should flow upward to the top of the head, creating an aura similar to Christ's halo or the topknot of the Buddha. If ch'i is blocked or uneven, the body will reflect it. For example, if you are constantly doubled over with a stomachache, eventually you will become permanently hunched over, reflecting improper ch'i flow in the body.

Experts look at the way you sit, move, and talk to discern the flow of ch'i in your system. Body movements, posture, facial expression, clearness of eyes, tightness of lips, skin tone, and speech cadence all reflect the direction and flow of ch'i. For example, bright and lively eyes indicate an active mind with many ideas.

The Chinese have long felt that ch'i can influence one's destiny and social interactions. (For specific character attributes and variations of human ch'i, see Appendix 2.)

Feng shui affects one's ch'i. After analyzing the flow of ch'i, an expert such as Lin Yun can use feng shui to help a person "untangle" knots that block happiness and attainment of one's goals and hopes.

There are limitations, however. The Chinese feel that each individual is born with good, medium, or bad luck, and that each individual has high and low phases. Cultivation of ch'i, however, can improve a medium-luck person's luck to be higher than that of a good-luck person who does nothing to develop his or her ch'i.

Human ch'i can be enhanced through a number of means: meditation, positive human relationships, and a healthy environment—good feng shui. While feng shui addresses all three ways of cultivating ch'i, this book deals primarily with surroundings: how to balance environmental ch'i flow to enhance and harmonize our own energy. (See Appendix 2 for meditations.) House ch'i and human ch'i have a lot in common. They both should flow smoothly. For instance, some people's ch'i is more attractive and we feel instinctively close to them. Other people's ch'i puts us off, and we avoid social contact with them. The ch'i of a house will also affect its atmosphere and therefore its occupants. In some places we feel comfortable, happy, and at home, and in others we feel anxious or depressed. Some places seem lively and bright. Others seem cold and dank and overbearing; these are all characteristics of a house's ch'i.

Moderation and enhancement of ch'i flow is the underlying aim of feng shui. Good ch'i flow in a dwelling improves the ch'i of residents. The concept of ch'i is essential for evaluating any home, office, or plot of land, and all their internal and external elements. Feng shui experts act like doctors of environmental ills, discerning ch'i circulation and pulse. They seek to create smooth, balanced, and fluid surroundings. For example, if three or more doors or windows are aligned in a row, they will funnel ch'i too quickly. A strategically hung wind chime will moderate ch'i flow. On the other hand, you should look out for the oppressive, constrained ch'i of a dark and narrow hall, which may depress and inhibit the occupant's chances for success in life and in work. Proper use of lights and mirrors will symbolically open up the space.

THE FIVE ELEMENTS

Along with yin and yang, the five elements are an additional way of analyzing and harmonizing the ch'i of a person or a house. Ch'i can be divided into five elements: metal, wood, water, fire, and earth. These powers, properties, and essences characterize all matter. The five elements can be associated with colors, times, seasons, directions, planets, body organs, and so on. (Feng shui uses the color cycle to adjust human ch'i (see Appendix 2). For example, water is associated with black—the deeper the water, the blacker it is—winter, and north; fire is red, summer, and south. These elements mutually create and destroy each other in a fixed order.

FIVE ELEMENTS

The five elements' color applications to the home will be explained later. When positioned in a harmonious area of a room or a building, these colors can adjust and enhance ch'i. For example, if a family is constantly arguing, something green placed near the center of the left wall may bring a truce. (See chapter 8 for symbolic areas of a room.)

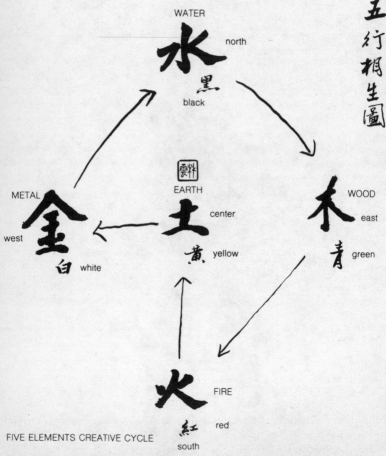

FIVE ELEMENTS CREATIVE CYCLE

In the creative cycle, fire produces earth (ash); earth creates metal (minerals); metal produces water (although water rusts metal, water droplets also form on the outside of a metal cup when holding cold liquid); water feeds wood; and wood helps fire.

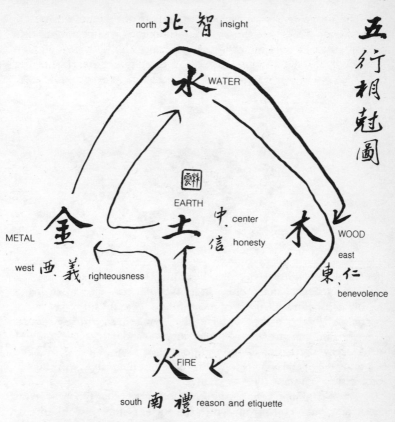

FIVE ELEMENTS DESTRUCTIVE CYCLE

In the destructive cycle, wood saps earth; earth obstructs water; water destroys fire; fire melts metal; and metal chops wood.

I CHING

The *I Ching* is a fundamental tool in feng shui's more mystical practices. The *I Ching* is the mother of Chinese thought. Growing out of early Chinese divination, it instructed emperors, priests, and scholars on the advisability of anything from waging war to taking a trip. It is a book in which divination and wisdom are imparted simultaneously. Its trigrams and hexagrams, while instructing on the appropri-

I CHING

ateness of an action, are also studies in the idea of yin and yang and constant cyclical change. They stress the connection between man's destiny and nature. Originally the trigrams were meant to represent the myriad things in the universe; they symbolized primary nature. The trigrams' lines are yin— — and yang———and in combination they make Heaven, Earth, Thunder, Mountain, Fire, Wind, Lake, and Water (see Appendix 3). They also represent the primal workings of Tao, and its constant state of change.

These trigrams were formed by tossing wooden blocks, yarrow stalks, and, later, coins from which the ancient Chinese would divine omens, instruction, and wisdom (The sixty-four hexagrams of the *I Ching* are all the possible combinations of the eight trigrams.)

Eventually the Chinese applied other meanings to the trigrams: family relations, directions, seasons, colors, parts of the body or face, parts of houses or rooms. The trigrams also came to symbolize eight fortunes or stages of life, ranging from patronage and help to happy marriages.

As a result, the Chinese used the *I Ching* not only for pure divination and philosophical purposes, but also as a highly charged mystical instrument. The *I Ching* appears in such diverse arts as face-reading, mystical medicine, palmistry, and, of course, feng shui.

In feng shui, an octagonal shape and its eight trigrams, called the *ba-gua,* is used as a mystical tool to diagnose environmental and life imbalances. It is a guide to improving health, happiness, and prosperity. The ba-gua shape is superimposed on the layout of a room, house, or plot to determine which area needs attention. For example, a corner jutting into the far right corner of a room may indicate marriage problems. A prescribed antidote—a strategically hung mirror—may make the relationship whole again. A house with a bathroom in the wealth area may find its finances flushed away.*

*Throughout this book, the ba-gua is used to interpret spaces and is described in detail in chapter 8. A full understanding of ba-gua interpretation will help you appreciate many of the other feng shui practices in this book.

3

SOLUTIONS

BUDDHIST HEART MAGIC CURES

According to Professor Lin, there are two ways to solve our problems: *ru-shr* and *chu-shr.* Ru-shr is logical, reasonable, and rational. It is that which is within our range of experience and knowledge. Within this book there are many rational, material, and sensible design solutions. But equally important are chu-shr cures—those that are illogical, irra-

RU-SHR

tional, transcendental, or mystical. Chu-shr is today's science fiction—
that which is still beyond our realm of experience and knowledge—
but, perhaps, tomorrow's fact.

With his own brand of irrationality, Professor Lin asserts that
ru-shr is, at best, 10 percent effective, while the positive outcome of
mystical chu-shr runs between 110 and 120 percent—meaning that
chu-shr cures not only resolve problem areas, but also enrich those
areas. For example, if a couple has marital problems, normal advice
is to be more patient, understanding, and loving. This is ru-shr—
logical, reasonable, and easy to accept. But as much as the couple
would like to respect and be considerate of each other and make the
marriage work, the results are only 10 percent effective. In using
chu-shr, the couple might only have to move their bed a few inches
to one side. This apparently irrational and illogical gesture—an act of
faith, perhaps, or the beginning of a subconscious healing process—
will enjoy far greater and more positive results than ru-shr.

The Black Hat sect of feng shui is still a mystery. Its ru-shr aspects
parallel many modern ideas of physics, medicine, and good design. Its
chu-shr approach encompasses the great expanse outside our known
world and within our subconscious: what is yet to be discovered,
understood, or seen.

The desired end result of chu-shr feng shui is to improve ch'i
flow. Indeed, the concept of channeling, balancing, and enhancing
ch'i is the whole purpose of feng shui. The logic behind this is that
when environmental ch'i is improved, this improves human ch'i,
bringing health, happiness, and good fortune.

CHU-SHR

CHU-SHR

To the extent that it can be categorized, chu-shr feng shui works through three basic techniques:

1. The *connecting ch'i method* taps into ch'i that is too far from a house or too deep beneath the earth's surface. A simple, stopgap variation is to plant into the earth a hollow pole with a light at the top to siphon up the ch'i. Another example: a house missing a corner seems incomplete; if there is a nearby detached shed, the construction of a pathway or loggia that connects the two buildings will symbolically make the house shape complete.

2. The *balancing ch'i* method brings the environment into harmony with itself and its surroundings. If a house is awkwardly shaped, a landscape or architectural feature might be added to achieve equilibrium. For example: a house with a garage that juts out to the left of the house makes residents who exit the house walk ten-odd steps to enter the garage. This will unbalance them; they will always "think left." Building a path or laying rocks to the right will balance the layout and symbolically open a new road and thus new opportunities.

3. The *outstanding method* can both increase and modify the flow of ch'i. The addition of a bright light, a fountain, or a bubbling fish tank can churn and activate weak or stagnant ch'i and help it circulate through a house. Strong, dangerous ch'i, on the other hand, can be dispersed by moving or musical gadgets, such as windmills, wind chimes, and bells. For example, if a wall is too close to the entrance

door, stifling ch'i and one's chances for growth, you can either hang a mirror on the wall to create a sense of depth, or install a bell or light that goes on when the entrance door is opened. This will make residents' ch'i rise so they won't be affected by the inhibiting wall.

THE NINE BASIC CURES

There are basic remedies to alter, moderate, or raise ch'i. Used both inside and outside a building, these cures can meet a number of needs: to resolve imbalances, to improve ch'i circulation, and to enhance one of the *I Ching*'s eight ba-gua areas and thus its corresponding life situation (see chapter 8).

THE NINE BASIC CURES

1. Bright or light-refracting objects: mirror, crystal ball, lights
2. Sounds: wind chimes, bells
3. Living objects: plants (real or man-made), bonsai, flowers, aquarium or fishbowl
4. Moving objects: mobile, windmill, whirligig, fountain
5. Heavy objects: stones or statues
6. Electrically powered objects: air conditioner, stereo, TV
7. Bamboo flutes
8. Colors
9. Others

Each cure has its particular qualities and uses; a windmill might disperse an oncoming road's "killing ch'i," while properly installed flutes might alleviate an overhead beam's oppressive effect.

Their specific attributes work as follows:

Bright Objects

Mirrors The so-called aspirin of feng shui, mirrors cure a host of feng shui woes, exterior or interior.

Outside a building, they deflect threatening ch'i, be it from a road that aims at it, an overpoweringly tall neighboring building, or a funeral parlor. The mirror both offensively reflects back malign ch'i and defensively provides protection. Any size will do. The mirrored glass walls used in contemporary architecture also help to deflect negative surroundings. Those wishing to remove the overbearing forces altogether might try a convex mirror, which reflects images upside-down. If a road aims at an entrance, hang the mirror above the door.

Inside a house or an office, mirrors serve many purposes. The general rule for interiors is "the bigger the mirror, the better." Mirrors should not cut off people's heads: if too short, they create headaches and lower residents' ch'i. If too high, they make residents uncomfortable. Mirrors should be hung in large pieces, not little mirror tiles that distort images. Properly hung to reflect good views of water or gardens to the interior, they draw in good outside ch'i, light, and scenery. In cramped quarters, a mirror can facilitate ch'i flow and create the illusion of expanse and light. Mirrors also reflect all intruders to anyone whose back is to the door. They can balance an L-shaped home or room. In business, if properly hung, they can increase profits.

Small-Faceted Crystal Balls These rounded prisms are prevalent in feng shui. Not entirely unlike the fortune-teller's smooth crystal ball, they are said to endow the occupant with the gift of farsightedness and a good perspective. They can adjust a home or office's ch'i, symbolically resolve design imbalances, and enhance ba-gua positions. As refractors of light or energy, they convert strong, threatening ch'i—both interior and exterior—and disperse it throughout the room. Thus they become symbolic sources of positive power and energy. (Hung in a western window, a crystal ball transforms the sun's glare into a rainbow of refracted colors.) They are also used both to improve ch'i flow symbolically and to lift up the home's ch'i, thereby improving the occupants' lives.

Crystal balls have special uses as ritual objects. Hung in a temple near the image of the Buddha, they acquire special powers. Blessed by a religious person with high spiritual energy, a crystal ball will convert light into power and energy, and a mantra and blessing will emanate from it and fill the room.

Lights Lights are powerful feng shui cures. Light itself is considered an important feng shui asset in any environment. Installed outside an L-shaped home, a lamp or floodlight can square off the missing corner. Installed at the lowest point of a hill, it can keep ch'i and money from rolling out of a sloped plot. Inside, lamps—symbolic of the sun and disseminators of energy themselves—can enrich interior ch'i. As a rule, the brighter the lamp, the better.

Sound

Wind Chimes Wind chimes are generally moderators of ch'i flow. They disperse malign interior and exterior ch'i, tempering and redirecting, say, a road or a hill's ch'i in a more beneficial, balanced way. Hung on eaves, they symbolically raise a house's ch'i. Wind chimes or bells can be used to summon positive ch'i—and money—into a home or business. Hung near an entrance, they act as alarms warning of intruders entering a room or a store. After a California bank was robbed in the mid-1970s, it installed, on the advice of a feng shui expert, a bell on the door to the tellers' work area that would ring each time the door was opened. As a primitive but effective security system, it seemed to unnerve any would-be robbers, because no holdups have occurred since then.

Living Objects

Plants and Flowers Plants—real, silk, or plastic; bonsai, annual, or perennial—not only symbolize nature, life, and growth, but also conduct nourishing ch'i throughout the room. They function in many ways. Plants indicate good feng shui; where a plant or a flower thrives, so will residents. Placed on either side of an entrance, they create and attract good ch'i. Inside and outside restaurants and stores, they are subtle beacons bringing in clients and money. Besides merely enlivening interior ch'i, plants can resolve design imbalances such as acute room angles, corners that jut into rooms, or unused storage space.

Man-made plants and silk flowers are effective substitutes indoors, because their leaves do not turn brown and petals do not fall off. Since artificial flowers are maintenance-free, residents—unless they have a green thumb—need not be confronted with symbols of death and age.

Fish Bowls and Aquariums These, like plants, are microcosms of nature, specifically the life-giving ocean. And water—essential to the cultivation of rice—symbolizes money. (The Chinese use the word *feng shui* [wind-water] as a slang term for gambling, i.e., "blowing away money.") So, when views of water are lacking, the Chinese use aquariums and fishbowls to evoke nourishing and money-making ch'i. Fish, the fruit of the sea, further enrich a home or office. In offices, fish are used to absorb accidents and general bad luck; when they die they are immediately replaced. Aquariums with bubbling aerators, which, like fountains, stimulate ch'i, are considered the most effective.

Moving Objects

Wind-powered or electrically powered moving gizmos such as mobiles (interior) and windmills, whirligigs, and weathervanes (exterior) also stimulate ch'i circulation and deflect the overbearing force of roads and long corridors.

Interior or Exterior Fountains or Man-made Geysers Fountains and geysers are also microcosms of ch'i-activating and money-producing water. They also can be protective; the strength of water disperses the "killing ch'i" of, say, an arrowlike road. Water fountains also create active, positive ch'i. In business they are used to encourage profits.

Heavy Objects

Stones or Statues Sometimes a heavy object, such as a stone or statue, when properly placed, can help stabilize an unsettling or elusive situation, be it holding down a job or holding on to a spouse.

Electrical Power

Machines powered by electricity are used to stimulate surroundings, for example, a television in the "career" area of a bar or equipment in the "helpful people" spot of a factory (see chapter 8).

Flutes

These have many symbolic and religious meanings. Historically, a bamboo flute was used to report peace and good news, and therefore, by association, its presence brings peace, safety, and stability to a home, office, or business. With its hollow, segmented interior, a bamboo flute symbolically lifts house ch'i, section by section. If two flutes with red ribbons tied around them are hung on a beam, slanting toward each other, thereby creating a partial ba-gua (octagonal) formation, they can pump ch'i upward from segment to segment and moderate the oppressive effect of the beam, allowing ch'i to penetrate it. (They must be hung with the mouthpieces at the lower ends.) Flutes are also protective. They symbolize swords and are hung in homes, restaurants, and stores to drive away evil spirits and would-be robbers. They also have ritual uses. When played, a flute strengthens weak home ch'i and generally boosts morale. When shaken, it drives away bad spirits.

Colors

Colors can be applied to areas in a room or a building to enhance aspects of one's life. The Chinese consider certain colors more auspicious than others. A feng shui expert praised an unusually decorated Chinese restaurant for its black interior because black is the color of the water element and therefore connotes money (see chapter 8). Yet, in general, black also signifies loss of light and is often avoided. Red, used in Chinese weddings and other celebrations, is an auspicious color. White, the Chinese color of mourning, is avoided. At Chinese funerals, relatives wear simple, unbleached muslin robes to express humble grief. Yellow, the color of the sun, represents longevity. Green, the color of spring, signifies growth, freshness, and tranquility. Blue is an ambiguous color, representing the sky. It is auspicious, yet sometimes, perhaps because of its coolness, blue represents death.

Others

Feng shui also uses a range of personal cures to address other problems. The cures are always increasing and changing to address new problems.

- Red ribbons for doors with knocking knobs
- Fringe to hide and resolve a slanted beam
- Chalk under the bed to cure a backache

—4—

SITING

EXTERIORS

According to feng shui, our position in the universe affects our destiny.

The theory underlying feng shui practice implies that when one is correctly and harmoniously positioned in the universe, both balance and harmony will bless one's life; when one is in flow with the powerful workings of nature and the cosmos, one's health, prosperity, and mental state will benefit. The re-creation of nature's patterns when siting a building or arranging its rooms and furniture will imbue the occupants with positive and balanced energy, and that energy will propel them along a fruitful and fortuitous life course. If, on the other hand, occupants are poorly placed—vis-à-vis the natural rhythms of the universe—their lives will be out of step, unbalanced, and a constant struggle.

Exterior elements—hill and river shapes, trees, and local landmarks, both natural and man-made—all contribute to determining the course of our lives. For example, we respond to good views—trees, flowers, or water—as well as to ugly or threatening formations—roads, corners, or poorly designed buildings. This chapter provides the basic principles of external feng shui and shows how exterior locations have a great impact on interiors.

NATURAL ELEMENTS

Although feng shui's origins remain obscure, it most likely began in early agrarian times, when farmers sought accommodation to and harmony with natural forces. Since ancient times, feng shui experts have been a special breed. I imagine they were early sages both keenly aware and observant of nature and possessing an astute knowledge of basic science. They knew to look at the base of a column for excess

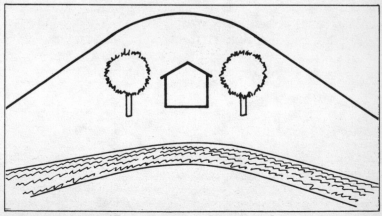

AN IDEAL FENG SHUI SITE

ground moisture, at the ring around the moon for weather forecasts, or even at the greenness and health of a plant for the fertility of an area. With observations such as these, they could correctly advise when and where to build a house. They combined this with psychology and a flare for the mystical—and the mysterious. In their pursuit of the most productive and blessed spots to live, they discovered that houses built halfway up a hill, facing south to the sea, fared best. There, shielded from harsh northern winds and protected from floods, with access to water and sun, crops and livestock thrived and residents were comfortable and relatively affluent. Their relative success, compared to that of their struggling neighbors, seemed to stem from the auspicious location and orientation of their homes. They saw it as the fortuitous tapping of the currents of wind and water, as well as the proper channeling of positive ch'i. Eventually, others imitated this arrangement, finding similar hills or settling near them. But when ideal circumstances were hard to find, early shamans used their skills to point the way, discerning and creating the luckiest spots available.

Eventually a feng shui theory evolved that ch'i circulates in the earth, spiraling around and around. Where it revolves near the surface, the land is fertile, the weather is mild, and the sun is warm. Trees and vegetables grow. The water and air are fresh and clear. People will be comfortable and happy. This is the best place to build a house. (When ch'i recedes from the surface, fruit, grass, and vegetables can't grow, and a desert results.) (See diagram.)

The purpose and principles of modern feng shui remain the same:

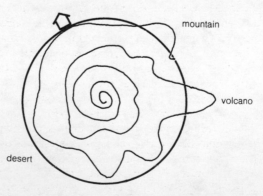

CH'I CIRCULATING IN THE EARTH

to find the best environment for a person to work and live up to his or her fullest potential. A feng shui expert will evaluate both the lay of the land and the earth's ch'i to site anything from a single-family house to large corporate offices.

Urban development, however, can interfere with feng shui. Outsiders who recognize a fortuitous area will build homes nearby. These new developments may block views or pollute a stream, changing positive attributes to negative ones. Here is where feng shui also comes into play. Instead of moving, suing, or tearing down homes and building higher ones, the Chinese have resorted to more subtle but effective solutions: chu-shr cures. For example, a mirror can be strategically hung facing an offending building, or a special ritual can be performed to recreate a positive atmosphere (see Appendix 1).

When choosing a plot of land or a house, feng shui experts consider its surroundings. For thousands of years, experts have deciphered signs and omens such as the color and size of a leaf, the prosperity of neighbors, or the general health of animals. The following are several ways to discern earth ch'i:

1. *Grass and plants:* If grass is green, ch'i is good and healthy. Brown, yellow, or bare spots on the lawn or field indicate ch'i flowing away from the surface. Look for "dragon points"—bright green areas where the vegetation is thick and flourishing—this is where to build.

2. *Lawn:* Lawns with thriving grass, flowers, and trees are signs of plentiful ch'i. Avoid buying land where there are sickly or dead plants or where flowers will not bloom.

3. *Animals:* Wild or domestic livestock on the premises are indications of good ch'i, and their health, demeanor, color, and sounds help feng shui experts evaluate the property. Good signs are a peaceful, pretty bird with colorful plumage and a beautiful song, or a cat with shiny thick fur. Crows and other squawking birds or mangy, wild dogs indicate bad ch'i. Deer, symbols of prosperity, are prized.

4. *Neighbors:* Residents often reflect earth ch'i. Lin Yun says that if your neighbors are prosperous and famous, you know ch'i is good. He points to Beverly Hills as an example that appealing, convivial neighborhoods generally attract successful people. On the other hand, if you want to rent a store and discover that the owners of nearby stores went bankrupt, took ill, died, had a car crash, or were recently divorced, or that across the street one store was robbed and another burned down, you might have second thoughts.

5. *Omens of bad ch'i:* These are forebodings of negative ch'i and bad luck, including even momentary happenings when visiting a site.

Be alert for lights that have burned out or explode when turned on, broken or stuck doors, a dead bird on the floor, a hearse that parks outside, even if only for the driver to pick up a sandwich at a nearby deli, and so on.

NATURAL EARTH SHAPES

Other considerations in siting a house or building are earth shapes. To the ancient Chinese, the earth and cosmos were one "living, breathing organism"*; nature was endowed not only with ch'i, but with human and animal characteristics. A mountain could be a dragon, an elephant, or a phoenix; an overhanging cliff a tiger's jaw. An entire branch of feng shui, the School of Forms, interprets the landscape by detecting shapes.

Dragons, the most frequent mountain metaphor in ancient China, were seen as awesome, benevolent guardians of villages and farmland. A series of ridges in a mountain's shape were vertebrae; foothills spread into arms and legs, streams and springs made up veins and arteries pumping the earth's ch'i, and correctly placed boulders were the dragon's eyes.

Another powerful natural force was the water dragon who inhabited the deep like a moody Loch Ness monster. He governed weather, tides, and water levels. When controlled, this dragon was the source of fertile fields; water itself became a symbol of money. When unchecked, he was the source of death and destruction.

Mountains and rivers—both manifestations of lively and nourishing ch'i—have always been crucial in the feng shui landscape. (Chinese landscape paintings are called *shan-shui,* literally "mountain-water.") Mountains were huge earth shields that protected cities and farms from harsh winds and barbarians that invaded from the north. Rivers were purveyors of crop-nourishing water.

Semi-divine emperors derived power from the balance of heaven and earth, mountains and rivers. Their destiny, and that of their subjects, was bound up with the unseen forces of nature. (A nation's destiny is called *shan-he,* literally "mountain-river.") Emperors consulted feng shui advisors before building large public works or waging wars. Their right to rule and the luck of the nation depended on their auspicious positioning between heaven and earth, which they be-

*Ernest Eitel. *Feng Shui: or the Rudiments of Natural Science in China* (Hong Kong, 1873), p. 20.

lieved brought abundant crops and successful military campaigns. A natural disaster, however, might portend the emperor's loss of the "mandate of heaven"—meaning he was out of sync with the natural powers—making him vulnerable to defeat. Nature, therefore, was carefully watched by imperial advisors such as generals, astrologers, diviners, and feng shui experts.

The earth-as-body concept of feng shui created a built-in precursor of latter-day environmental concerns. Feng shui experts sought out ch'i, the earth's pulse, as though they were the earth's physicians, tapping into the vital energy of the universe. The Chinese took care when altering the earth's flesh. They took great pains to avoid tampering with or unbalancing the earth's ch'i or rupturing a dragon's vein. The Great Wall is a classic example. From beginning to end, it covers eleven hundred miles as the crow flies. But it is actually twice that long. It was built twisting and turning along every earthly deviation to avoid rupturing the earth, and thus the stability of the Ch'in Dynasty (221–207 B.C.) China.

For the same reason, feng shui was the bane of nineteenth-century Western missionaries and businessmen; they complained that it interfered with missionary zeal and dampened capitalist dreams. Feng shui was invoked by local Chinese to ban Christian church crosses— they were said to impale the earth—as well as to prevent the construction of railroads, the installation of telegraph lines, and the establishment of a lumber industry. According to feng shui, all tampered with the harmony of the earth.

When the Chinese themselves ignored feng shui's tenets, they suffered as a result. Centuries of deforestation in northern China have allowed heavy rains to erode the fertile soil, leaving arid land in their wake.

Mountains

In rural and suburban settings, earth shapes, whether mountains, hills, or plots of land, are still considered outcroppings of ch'i. Hillsides are the most desirable places to live; flat, featureless land, regarded as devoid of good ch'i, is avoided. In ancient China, when hills were not available, they were created. Man-made berms not only enhanced both the landscape and the area's feng shui, but also were practical, holding in the heat in winter and remaining cool in the summer. Hills acted as huge earth shields, and if a house was built at the foot of a hill, trees were planted as additional protection.

In general, mountains are examined in three regular forms: round, square, or triangular. The gentle contour of a rounded hill rolling into a river valley is preferable. Less desirable is a house atop a square butte. While it is protected from floods, it is exposed to strong winds. Protection—against wind, water, western sun, neighboring houses, arrowlike roads—is a recurring concern in feng shui. An armchair-shaped hill or mother-embracing-child formation provides good protection for the house on three sides—even better if a lower hill rises in front like a footstool.

This classic feng shui arrangement is traditionally described as a sort of mountain menagerie: the house is protected from the northern wind by the black tortoise mountain in back; the white tiger to its right blocks the malign western sun glare; the green dragon to the left guards the site if the ferocious white tiger gets out of hand; the red phoenix in front is low enough to allow a vista but high enough to protect the site and its occupants (see diagram).

If the hill is irregular, symbolic interpretation and manipulation of the shape can create good luck. For example, living on or near a hill that looks like a calligrapher's brushrest is auspicious for those with scholarly, social, and political aspirations; passing imperial exams was once a way for even a poor clerk to achieve high rank in government. Other auspicious mountain shapes can be seen to resemble, for example, a lion's head or the face of a bodhisattva. Use these symbolic interpretations to your advantage.

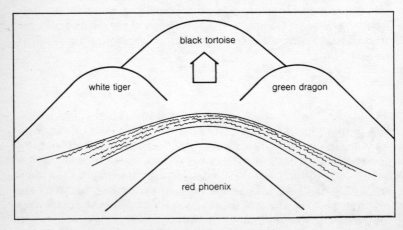

ARMCHAIR-AND-OTTOMAN ARRANGEMENT OF MOUNTAINS

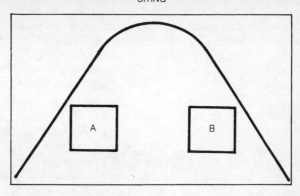

A TRIANGULAR HILL

If a hill is triangular and looks like a clamshell, buy lot A or B, which rests on the muscle of the shell, holding in ch'i and money.

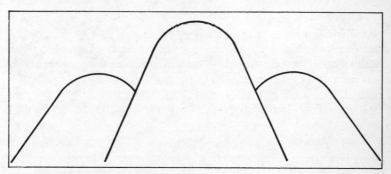

CALLIGRAPHER'S BRUSHREST MOUNTAIN SHAPE

When an oddly shaped mountain doesn't bring any auspicious associations to mind, you can alter the shape slightly to create good fortune. By resolving an odd shape, you create the best situation of all. For example, if a hill resembles a headless dragon's body, a house built at the neck will complete the animal, bringing harmony and wholeness to the area and improving both its own and its residents' ch'i. The house also positions occupants in the thought and control area. (See following illustration.)

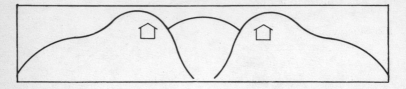

TWO-DRAGON MOUNTAINS

These hills create two dragons playing with a pearl. To encourage good fortune, build a house near or install light posts on the dragons' eyes.

MOUNTAINS

The illustrations opposite show a selection of hill shapes:

1. As a rule, avoid steep, abrupt hills and slopes that conduct ch'i too quickly and can cause mudslides.

2.–4. Gentle grades are best; these are good slopes to build on, and provide good drainage.

5. Build on the flatter side (house on right), never on the top of the hill, or on the cliff (house on left).

6. House orientation is an important consideration. A house that backs on a mountain and looks out down a gentle slope is desirable. Placement of houses on slopes numbered 2, 3, 4, and 6 are good if the house faces away from the hill. A house facing a hill will be bad for the occupants' wealth and careers. A road running in front of the house higher than the house confounds this problem.

CURE. If a house faces a mountain and the backyard is a garden, place a spotlight in the back of the garden and shine it toward the top of the house, or install a flagpole at the rear of the garden to balance ch'i.

7. Do not build above or below an overhang, an unstable formation known as a tiger's jaw, or the beast will gobble up your luck. When building on a flatter slope, it is best to build a low house with only one or two stories. A very tall building will be oppressive to land ch'i. Also, avoid building on top of a steep hill.

Rivers

A house sited near to and with a view of water will thrive, as a rule. Ideally, the house faces the pond, river, or sea.

The analysis of rivers—the lifelines and links of early Chinese settlements—has long been an art. Potentially nourishing to crops and to commerce and potentially devastating to farms and homes, their configurations raised much speculation. A meandering river was most desirable, as it could irrigate a wider swath of land. A straight river or one with sharp bends is dangerous; with nothing to regulate its fast current, ch'i flows too quickly past an area to enrich it.

The *quality* of water is also important. It should be alive—clean and active, a sign of vital, pure ch'i—not dead. Stagnant and murky water indicates tainted ch'i and money.

CURE. To attract distant water hang a mirror, which, like a magnet, draws in ch'i and money-making opportunities. A New York graphic artist found that a month after hanging a mirror over his bed to draw in the waters of the Hudson River, he received a 40-percent raise in a job he had started only three months before.

The illustrations opposite show that different river formations affect a house's feng shui in a variety of ways.

1. First, check which direction the house faces and how close the house is to the water. If the house faces the river, this is good and the family will enjoy wealth. A house facing away from the river is less fortuitous; residents will see opportunities but will not be able to grasp them.

CURE. Install a mirror inside the house facing the river to draw in the river's positive ch'i.

Ideally, the distance between the house and the river is twice the house's height. If the house is small, the home's foundation may be undermined both literally and figuratively. The family will be overwhelmed by the river ch'i and bothered by illness. If the house is large and high, it is considered well balanced with the river.

2. Residents of the house will enjoy wealth, especially if the house is facing the river. The house is embraced by water, which symbolizes money.

3. If the river inverts away from the house, residents can see possible profits, but will never be able to acquire them (unlike an ocean bay).

CURE. Install a mirror inside the house to reflect the water.

4. A house facing a waterfall brings good fortune.

5. The direction of a river's flow is another important consideration. A river flowing toward the house's front door is good. However, if it predominantly flows away, the residents will suffer financial losses. (Sometimes it is necessary to consult a feng shui expert—or a map—to discern the river's course.)

6. An auspicious river configuration, as if it embraced the home.

7. This river configuration is unstable, making residents' finances uneven. On one hand, they can see success; on the other, they cannot reach it (the inverted river). Yet the embracing river bestows luck. So a person living there will have to struggle, but in the end he will succeed.

8. A good configuration is to be sited above a confluence of streams with an island in front, especially if the house is backed by a gentle hill. A steep hill, however, can harm occupants' luck.

9. This house is sited in a good location because it is embraced by a river bend.

10. A house in a bay is best; money will flow in. Though a house sited on a peninsula can be good for family wealth, it should not be overly exposed to the elements, or money will be hard to hold on to.

RIVERS

11. This river can be either lucky or unlucky, depending on the direction of its flow. If it flows toward the house, it bodes well, but less well if it flows away. Yet even this is better than having no water at all.

12. This can be a good configuration if the water flows toward the house, and not as good if it flows away.

13. The house is threatened by this river. If, however, the water is merely a man-made canal and quite docile, the house will enjoy good luck.

THE MAN-MADE LANDSCAPE

As civilization grew and, of necessity, man's hand shaped the landscape with roads and buildings, new feng shui problems arose, and from them grew rules for harmonizing the environment. Often old rules proved adaptable to modern times. Roads and driveways convey ch'i in a manner similar to rivers; meandering routes are best. Buildings and plot shapes are given the symbolic attributes of mountains; neighboring buildings towering over a house are threatening, or a land plot may be interpreted as clam-shaped.

However, siting a house is no longer merely a question of mountains and rivers, wind and water. Artificial barriers and shapes—roads, plot shapes, neighboring buildings, trees, driveways—all have a major impact on residents. Yet, in urban and suburban settings, the principles of balance, moderation, and enhancement of ch'i still govern feng shui rules and cures.

Land Plots

Square and rectangular plots are preferable. But height, width, and degree and direction of slope are also considered. Even on a mountain, a level plot is better than a sloped one. As a rule, if the plot slopes, site a house on the higher portion of the plot rather than on the lower area. However, when the ground slopes down from a house, ch'i, opportunity, and money can roll out.

CURE. To balance the highs and lows of this uneven ground, install a lamp or spotlight to cycle ch'i and money back.

Avoid tops of hills, which can expose a house to harsh winds. Trapezoid-shaped lots ideally have their narrower end at the rear. This provides a strange mixed metaphor: its "dust bin" shape collects good

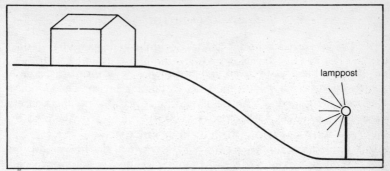

HOUSE ON SLOPE

ch'i, which is swept in. It can also be seen as a clamshell plot, so the house should be built in the clam's muscle to hold in ch'i and money.

If it is narrower in front, residents' future will get narrower and narrower.

CURE. Create a curve in the front using flowers, a brick path, or a driveway, so that the shape resembles a money bag.

Irregularly shaped plots are even more challenging for a feng shui expert. The inconsistent form, however, can be enlivened and made auspicious through creative manipulation. Unusual-shaped lots can be unsettling for residents, so the "balancing method" can be applied to correct the imperfections. For example, with the unusual shape at the top of page 41, a lamppost and hedges complete the shape, making it more solid and creating a resemblance to a scorpion, thus adding to residents' power. (See following illustration).

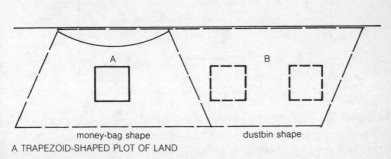

A TRAPEZOID-SHAPED PLOT OF LAND

If narrower in front, create a curve in front using flowers and bricks or a driveway to make it resemble a money bag, thus collecting money and ch'i.

If the plot is wider in front, resembling a shell, build the house on the muscle of the shell to hold money and ch'i.

Positioning a House on a Land Plot

A building's relationship to the road creates the juncture through which opportunity, wealth, and health enter a house. The distance between the road and a house should be at least half of the house's front-to-back length. Otherwise, occupants will be overwhelmed by the road and will have to struggle in all enterprises.

CURE. Install a floodlight or a fountain between the house and the road, sending ch'i upward. Other methods include adding a small windmill to the roof or, less effective, hanging a wind chime or mirror on the house.

The house's position should complement the plot. A house nested in the middle one-third of the plot creates the most balanced situation. The rearmost one-third is preferable to the front one-third. CURE. If the house is not in the middle of the plot, plant a tree or install a lamppost or heavy stone at the opposite end of the plot to balance the house.

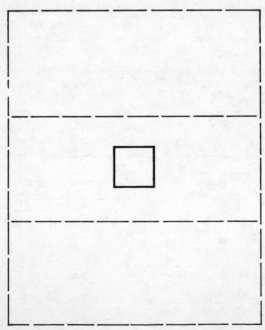

Ideal position for a house on a plot.

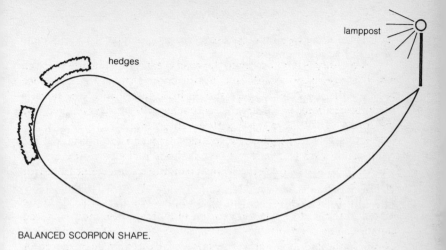

BALANCED SCORPION SHAPE.

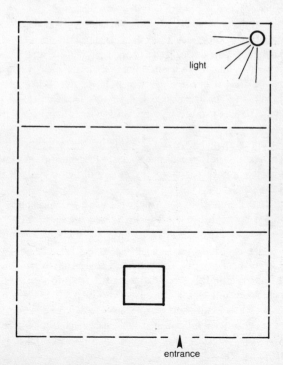

An unbalanced house position on a plot is resolved by a lamp.

The following illustrations explain a variety of land plots and where to position houses on them.

Land plot shapes.

1. A circular plot provides many opportunities to develop and advance in life. It is like the hub of a wheel from which all things radiate. If the house is built in a square shape at the center of the lot —resembling ancient Chinese money—residents' finances will be exceptionally good.

2. A square plot generally is good. If, however, the house lies in the front half of the lot, residents' luck will start out well, but eventually will turn sour. It is best to locate the house in the center of the lot for a more balanced life, a successful career, and growth in prosperity.

CURE. Install spotlights in the center of the back of the lot and in each front corner (see chapter 8 on the Three Harmonies) and shine each light at the top of the roof.

3. A rectangle is basically the same as a square. If the house is in the front half of the plot, use the cure for squares above.

4. This shape, with a rounded front, is provident and has growth potential; it will attract money and success. If the plot is rounded in back and the house sits in the center or back of the lot, residents will lead a balanced life. If the house lies in the front third of the lot, occupants will have unstable careers and will fall prey to frequent illness.

5. A rhombus is good. A house built in the middle or the front section of the lot will help residents' careers to develop quickly. If the house is in the back part, residents' careers will be stable, but will not develop as quickly.

6.–7. A house in a diamond-shaped lot is fine if it is parallel with the sides and if the entrance to the lot is not on a corner.

CURE. If the house is oriented toward an angle, balance it with a tall tree, flagpole, or floodlight in back of the house. Otherwise, residents may have lawsuits, accidents, or even full-scale disasters.

8. It is undesirable for a door to face an angle in a triangular lot. The house door should face a flat side. The best place for a house is in the muscle of this simplified clam shape to hold in money. If the house is in the center and faces the angle, residents' financial road will narrow and abruptly end. The next generation will also fail; no hope for success.

CURE. Install a flagpole or a plant to offset and hide the corner.

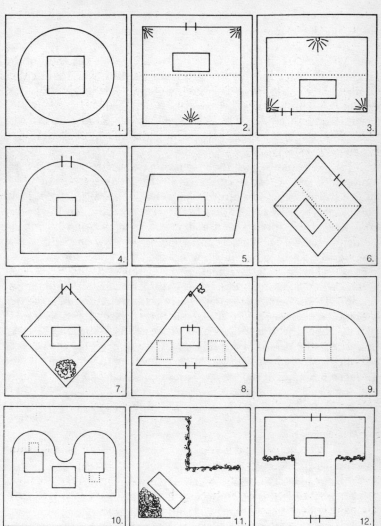

PLOT SHAPES

9. A semicircular plot is very good, especially if the house is built in the middle to imitate half of a Chinese coin.

10. With a lot shaped like a camel's back, the house should be built in the center, if the center is sufficiently wide. (The front of the plot must be twice as wide as the house's height.) A house in either of the humps is bad. If sited in the left hump, the family will suffer, and in the right hump, children will have problems.

CURE. Build an addition in the "family" (left-hump cure) or the "children" (right-hump cure) section of the master bedroom. (See chapter 8.)

11. An L-shaped plot or a lot missing a corner can be inauspicious, as though a section of the residents' lives were missing.

CURE. If a house is not already built, site it askew from the main corner, and at least twenty feet from the corner. Behind the house, plant a tall tree or install a lamp and plant something along the missing corner so success will come despite the unfortunate shape. A house built square on the plot will bring drastically unstable fortunes, fluctuating suddenly from extremely good to very bad.

CURE. When breaking ground, mix a teaspoon of ju-sha with ninety-nine drops of wine in a rice bowl with uncooked rice. Sprinkle the rice around the perimeter. Use the Three Secrets (see Appendix 1).

12. Check where the entrance is located in T-shaped plots. An entrance in the base of the stem helps boost careers, but discourages learning, and residents will find others unwilling to help them. If the entrance is along the bar of the T, residents' marriages and finances will suffer.

CURE. Plant vines along the underside of the bar.

Roads

Roads, like rivers, purvey ch'i. Gently curved streets and parkways that follow natural contours are best suited for carrying smooth ch'i flow. Straight avenues and superhighways conduct ch'i too quickly and are potentially dangerous. This is known as arrowlike or "killing" ch'i. Traditionally, homes situated at the ends of dead-end streets are targets for killing ch'i and are less desirable than houses flanking the street. Being in the line of fire of the road's arrowlike ch'i will expose residents to bright headlights of oncoming traffic—like eyes of tigers stalking in the night.

CURE. Hang a mirror above the door, aiming at the road. Or install a fountain or an arrow-shaped whirligig between the road and the house.

Driveways

A driveway is also an important conduit of ch'i, linking a home to the main artery of a road. A smooth, meandering, and relatively level approach from the road is best, filtering out bad exterior ch'i. A semicircular driveway also is good. Pay attention to the way you enter and exit. Make sure the direction of your exit follows the prevalent traffic flow of the main road. If the road leads to the city, exit the drive on the city side of the semicircle and enter it on the country or suburban side. Here are some variations:

A forklike driveway in front of the door means father and son will quarrel and the house will be in discord; each wants to go on his own way.

CURE. Paint red dotted lines or lay bricks like dashes across the driveway or path.

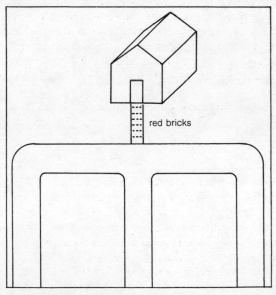

red bricks

A FORKLIKE DRIVEWAY

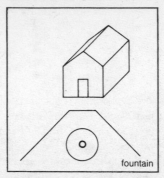

AN OCTAGONAL DRIVEWAY

A ba-gua (octagonal) structure in front of a house is bad for the relationship between generations. (The door is in the house's "water" position and the foot of the driveway end is in the "fire," spot, creating a mutually destructive relationship. See chapter 8).
CURE. Install a lamp, a tree, a fountain, flowers, or a windmill in the circle.

A driveway that narrows at the foot signifies dwindling career and financial opportunities. The worst of all situations is if it slopes down so steeply that you can't see the foot.
CURE. At the narrowest point, install a lamppost spotlighted at the door, or at the top of the roof, to recycle opportunities. If the driveway slopes, install two brick posts near the bottom to recirculate ch'i. If the road slopes down to the house, install a lamp behind the house to recycle ch'i to the highest point of the roof.

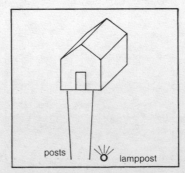

A TAPERING DRIVEWAY

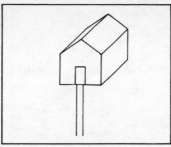

A NARROW DRIVEWAY

If the path is narrower than the width of the main door, not enough ch'i will enter the house, and the residents' luck will be stifled. CURE. Widen the path to enhance ch'i flow.

Circular driveways in front of a home are best. If the center is planted with grass or flower beds, family wealth will grow. Though this arrangement is highly unlikely, the ideal driveway is nine or ten circles or squares in a row. The sequence symbolizes Chinese coins— or hidden wealth. Ten circles enclosing squares represent the ten emperors of the Ch'ing Dynasty. A string of ten coins is a ritual object to ward off evil—invoking the power of all Ch'ing emperors. In addition, a square within a circle—the design of coins—symbolizes money and cosmic unity of Tao. (Heaven is round and earth is square.)

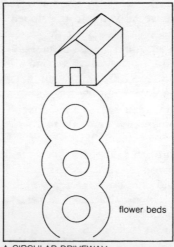

flower beds

A CIRCULAR DRIVEWAY

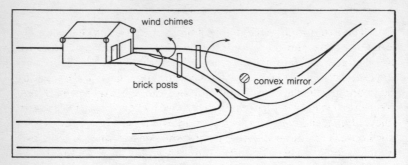

DRIVEWAY IN HILLSBOROUGH WITH CURES

This Hillsborough, California, home, which is vulnerable to currents of strong ch'i from a public road aimed at it, exhibits a selection of cures. The driveway slopes down to the road, allowing good ch'i and opportunity to roll away. The cure that the owner devised solves both problems: she installed two brick posts on the sides midway up the driveway to overcome strong ch'i and stop good ch'i from flowing away from the house down the driveway. She then hung wind chimes on four corners of the roof to lift the ch'i of the house and to further disperse the road's strong ch'i.

In the Forbidden City, the emperors' domain in Peking, wind chimes were hung on sloped eaves of many buildings as a protection. Traditionally, upcurved roofs were also for protection. It was said that devils could drop from heaven and the sloped roofs would deflect them, sending them skyward, and if the demons dared to pounce again, the spiked eaves would impale them. Folklore aside, the sloped roofs were designed for practical reasons: to allow maximum winter sun exposure and to keep out the hot summer sun. Roofs are more sloped in the south to block out the sun, and less sloped in the north to allow wind to flow easily over the house. The little beasts that ornament many Chinese eaves are said to guard against fires, ghosts, and thieves.

In the Hillsborough home, the acute angle a car exiting the driveway must turn also created a dangerous and unsmooth situation that ultimately would unbalance residents' ch'i. The owner installed a convex mirror to aid visual access and reflect continuity with the road and allow smooth ch'i flow. "I can see the house in the mirror," she comments. "It is as though the ch'i is drawing me in."

Entrance/Exit

The exterior entrance to a building—the threshold between the home or office and the outside world—is a key factor in feng shui. While traditional feng shui has stressed the orientation of a main door, Black Hat sect use of feng shui concentrates on how the various surroundings leading up to the entrance can affect occupants' lives. The entrance provides a prelude to how we feel once we have entered the building, and determines how we approach the world after we exit the house. The entrance should be gracious and accessible and the exit should present a clear, unobstructed view and pathway. Remove obstacles close to the door, such as columns, trees, walls, or utility poles, which will hinder ch'i flow and block good health and opportunities for wealth. The presence of a tree or plant at a safe distance from the entrance, however, often serves as good protection.

Pathways have a similar effect. If the path is close to the house, but very narrow, residents' ch'i will be inhibited and unbalanced. CURE. Either widen the path and avoid planting tall or bushy trees or shrubs near it, or hang a wind chime in front of the door.

Here are some more examples:

1.–2. As a rule, the best entrances give an open, spacious, even grand feeling. Paths leading from the building should open out.

3. A narrow path will limit career and financial prospects. If a house sits on a slope, a downhill facing entrance is better than an uphill facing door.

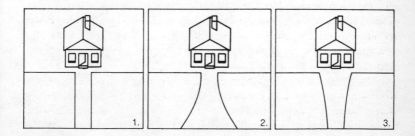

ENTRANCES

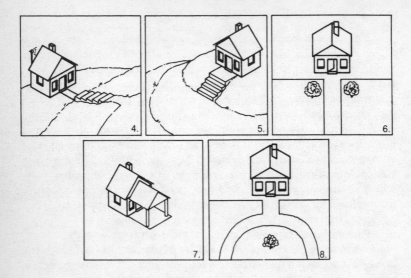

4.–5. If there are steps, they should be gradual and not too steep. The door should open on a wide landing. Narrow, steep steps allow money to roll out of the house. Steps that lead down to a house are bad. Residents will find their careers uphill battles. To remedy this, install a spotlight or a lamp aimed at the roof.

6. Bushes and shrubs are good, enhancing the ch'i of the house. They should be healthy and allow the walkway to be spacious; if the bushes are overgrown, trim them back.

7. While porches can provide gracious approaches and additions to houses, be careful of obstructive pillars. Columns and pillars should not be too big and close to the door. Round columns are better than square, which can cause bankruptcy. To resolve a square column, grow vines up the edges. An oppressive pillar can be cured by a mirror installed at eye level, or the words "When exiting, receive blessings" written on it.

8. Paths leading to the door can be curved. An even arc is desirable, as are plants between the sides.

Trees

Trees and foliage further improve the feng shui landscape. They serve many important functions. When planted as a hedge, they protect against killing ch'i—malign winds or traffic noise and pollution. They can also shield a house from a multitude of ominous sights, such as graveyards, churches, or arrowlike roads that aim directly at the house. On a hill, trees and bushes prevent erosion of rich soils or even mudslides. As a living entity, a tree's mere presence improves the ch'i of a plot or an area. Plants with vibrant green leaves are signs of good, nurturing ch'i. Trees also represent the life-force of the residents. Evergreens—traditional symbols of longevity—are preferable to deciduous trees, which in winter seem dead.

Trees can be used to balance an awkward plot or building shape. If a building is L-shaped, for instance, a tree can symbolically square off the structure, thus making it whole. Trees can also bring harmony to a plot of land that is too large for a house. However, if trees are poorly placed, directly in front of a house's entrance or window, they can be destructive and oppressive. This inhibits the flow of incoming ch'i and harms the ch'i of residents.

CURE. While some Chinese write characters of good luck—"When exiting, receive blessings"—on obstructive trees at eye level, to greet them with good luck when they exit, a ba-gua mirror will also work well by symbolically penetrating the tree's oppressive qualities. Avoid planting foliage with thorns or spiny leaves near walkways.

As one of the Nine Basic Cures, trees are often used to offset imbalances in a landscape or a house shape. The following illustrations show how trees can improve—and at times harm—a landscape.

1. The presence of this tree is good. The position of the entrance to the house and the driveway will determine what area of a person's life is enhanced by the tree. If the entrance is on side A, the resident will be famous; on side B, the family will thrive; on side C, careers will be successful; and on side D, the children will prosper (see chapter 8).

2. It is advisable, in general, to have a tree behind a house, especially if the house backs on to a mountain. As the tree grows, the home will enjoy increased stability, and residents' lives will steadily improve.

3. These trees are particularly important when they protect the house from reminders of death. When sited across from a church, a home can accumulate bad luck emanating from funerals and memorial services. Unshielded by trees, the inhabitants are vulnerable to illness, misfortune, and sudden, unexpected adverse events. This is caused by excess yin ch'i.

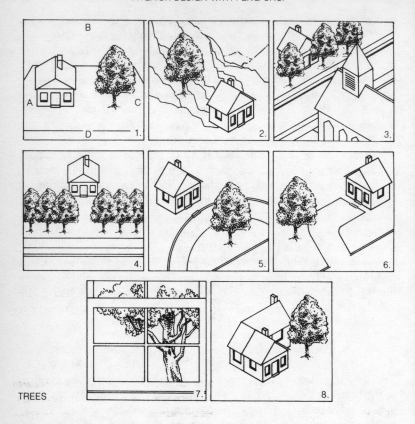

TREES

4. This configuration is good, as though the trees are standing guard on the property. They ward off the ill effects of an outside road. Flourishing, healthy trees should be planted in rows of 3, 6, or 9. A dead tree symbolizes the decay of residents' ch'i. Indeed, trees can represent your luck and destiny. If a tree dies, it foretells a sad event; you may suffer hardship or have an accident or even a death in the family.

5. This tree is good for residents if it is not oppressively close to the house. If a road points directly at the house, the tree shields the house from killing ch'i. Again, proportion is important. If the tree is too big or too close, it cannot counterbalance the ill effects of the road. The arched driveway is a lucky shape for residents and can solve the problems of an oppressive tree if the driveway is wide

enough to provide enough separation between house and tree.

6. This postion is also good for family and career, if the tree is not too close to the entrance to overshadow it.

7. A tree should not be planted too close to the window. If no sun gets through, residents may suffer. Not only does it thwart ch'i flow in the home, but also the tree, rooted in earth (yin), brings up too much yin ch'i. If the sun (yang) shines through, the yin ch'i is counterbalanced. If the tree gives you a sense of beauty, it is good. If it seems oppressive and blocks a good view, it is bad.

CURE. Hang five firecrackers—or imitations—on the window frame.

8. Trees can resolve the shape of a house when one or more corners are missing. Without the presence of this tree, the residents would find others unwilling and unable to help them (see chapter 8). When trees are cut down or chopped to the stump, this may affect the lives, limbs, and teeth of residents, unless they follow this cure: Plant ivy and wrap the stump with the green leaves as it grows. When cutting a tree, mix one teaspoon of ju-sha with ninety-nine drops of newly opened liquor, flick the mixture around the tree using the Three Secrets, and you will be protected against injury to limbs, bones, and teeth (see Appendix 1).

Ponds

Ponds or pools also affect feng shui. A pond or any body of water on or near a property is good. Ponds will help owners reach new levels of prosperity. Owners should take care that the water—symbolic of money—is kept clean and fresh, and better yet stocked with fish. Muddy, stagnant water implies tainted, ill-gained profits; fish bring good luck.

The size and placement of a pond should be balanced within the plot of land. It should be close enough to the house for residents to benefit from the water's ch'i. If it is too close or too large, however, the house will be overwhelmed by strong blasts of ch'i causing all sorts of misfortune. The overdose of yin ch'i and dampness causes skin and lung problems, as well as weakening residents' ch'i so they will have difficulty succeeding in their careers.

CURE. To lengthen the distance of an uncomfortably close body of water, lay a winding path from the pond to the house. To tone down a large pool, either install a lamp or a rock garden or plant a tree on the other side of the house opposite the pond. This balances and

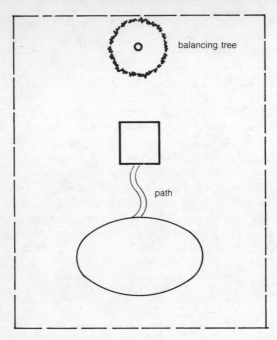

Cures for a pond that is too close to or too large for a house.

extends the house's domain and disperses the malign effects of the pond's strong ch'i.

Swimming pools follow pond rules. Kidney shapes curving toward the house are best. If the pool is rectangular, avoid having an angle point toward the house. Here are some examples.

1. Residents will be fortunate and well known, especially if they balance the strong influence of the pond with two spotlights aiming back at the house.

2. Residents will find many people anxious to help them.

3. Two ponds on a property should be the same size.
CURE. Build a bridge connecting them.

4. This situation is similar to number 1 but the size of pond number 4 is in balance with the corresponding house and bodes well for finances and fame.

5. With a pond that curves away from the house, residents will have money, but will constantly lose it—money drains away.

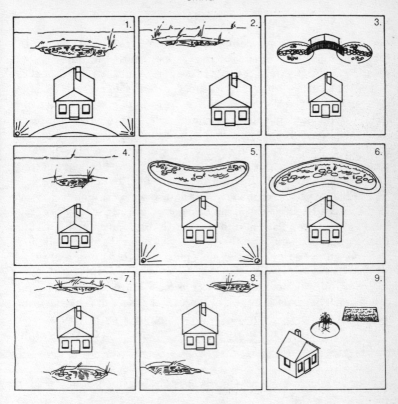

PONDS

CURE. Install spotlights in corners aimed to shine back at the house's roof.

6. The best pond form is crescent-shaped and wraps toward the house as if in an embrace. The home will enjoy much wealth; money is held in, and careers will be well developed.

7. Residents will have good careers and much renown.

8. Occupants will enjoy a good marriage and scholarly success. Do not build an island or gazebo in the pond to the right, or when one spouse spends time at home, the other will be away.

9. If a pond or swimming pool is angular or rectangular with a corner pointing at the house, residents will be sick or lose money. CURE. Install a fountain or plants to protect the house from the angle.

CITYSCAPE

Although urban feng shui tries to follow traditional country or suburban rules—park views of trees, water, grass, and hills, not to mention landscaped terraces, are best—nature usually plays a smaller role in the auspiciousness of a city site. City feng shui presents a whole new set of concerns. Man-made features—buildings, bridges, and streets—tend to dominate the natural elements: high-rises replace mountains, roads replace rivers. Neither the weight of a skyscraper crushing an earth dragon nor a superhighway cutting into its flesh seem of much concern. An urban dweller will more likely be affected by the traffic flow and direction of a road than by the current and configurations of a river. (Some feng shui rules pertaining to natural elements can be applied to man-made structures. In a high-rise, the ideal spot for a resident is on the middle floors, high enough to avoid street noise, headlights, and the oppressive weight of upper floors, and low enough to be free of buffeting winds—an urban version of siting a home halfway up a mountain.)

As a result, urban feng shui experts must address more than wind and water. They must channel, enhance, and deflect ch'i coming from a new set of physical considerations, ranging from pedestrian and vehicular traffic flow to tall shadows and sharp corners cast by neighboring skyscrapers.

Urban Homes and Offices

Urban homes and offices can fall victim to malign forces such as neighboring funeral homes, toweringly oppressive buildings, or adjacent building corners that may point in a threatening manner. One traditional feng shui expert in New York claims that a corner of the Trump Tower pointing at the new AT&T building may wreak havoc on the corporation, unless AT&T properly defends itself with an appropriately blessed ba-gua mirror.

Roads

Worst of all are roads—such as a dead end or perpendicular street—aiming at a building like an arrow. Such is the case with the White House, which stands in the line of 16th Street's "killing ch'i." In this case, it is bad not only for the President and First Lady themselves, but also for the nation. The arrowlike road causes national divisiveness and blasts away the area's positive ch'i. The President, as a result, cannot govern to his fullest potential.

CURE. Although some of the negative energy of oncoming roads is offset by the trees in Lafayette Park, it would be more effective to install a large fountain to disperse the ch'i. A simpler cure is a mirror or an arrow-shaped weather vane aiming at the road.

Similarly, a bridge that points directly at the house will cause health, personal, and financial problems.

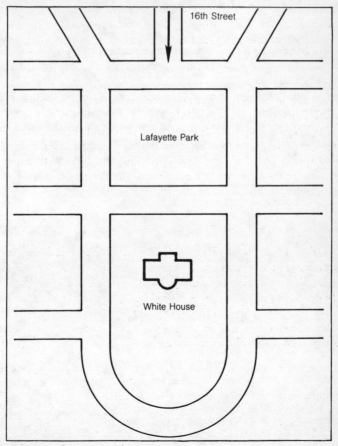

THE WHITE HOUSE

Neighbors

Once settled into what may be a perfect site, residents must still be on the alert for developments that may change and unbalance the harmony of the area. The shape, angle, height, and nature of adjacent buildings can affect a home. The following illustrations offer a variety of cures.

1. In this situation, where a neighboring high-rise dwarfs the home, occupants' ch'i will be oppressed by the height and shadow of the overbearing larger building. As a result, their careers, personal growth, and prosperity will be stunted.
CURES.

- A hexagonal mirror hung in an apartment or out of the window facing the offending building will reflect back its overshadowing qualities.
- A pool of water or a small mirror placed on the smaller building's roof will both deflect back the towering building's overbearingness and reflect it in the water in a horizontal position—as if it had symbolically collapsed. As an added benefit, the pool's water encourages the ch'i of the occupant's building to rise and circulate.
- Hang a convex mirror aimed at the large building, reflecting the high-rise upside down.

2. There are a variety of precautions for a home or an office facing an institution. A school is the least malign institution to face, although it is not an ideal situation. A church or temple is fine if mostly marriages take place there, or if the church is used as a seminary. But if the church is used mostly for funerals and memorial services, the residents will absorb too much yin ch'i—the ch'i of the dead—and sudden, unforeseen disasters may befall them.
CURE. Plant trees to block out the yin ch'i, or seal the doors (see Appendix 1.)

3. When a road separates your house from a larger building, first analyze the street's width. If the street is wide enough, i.e., three or four times the height of your house, there will be little effect from the larger building. If the street is narrow, your house and luck will be overshadowed by the building. In that case, use the mirror or water on the roof (as advised in number 1). A corner of a neighboring

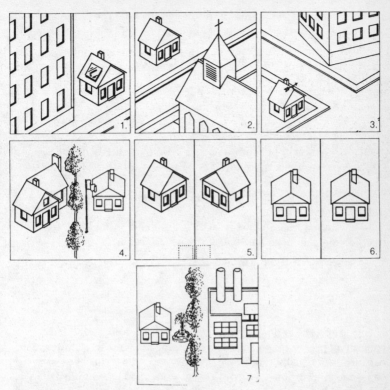

NEIGHBORS

building that points at your home or office can threaten your luck and chances of success. It can also expose you to accusations, acts of violence, and possible surgery.

CURE. Hang a mirror on the façade of your building, or install a whirligig or weathervane with an arrow pointing at the sharp corner. For example, on the advice of an expert, a Canadian businessman in Hong Kong protects himself from a menacing building across the street. He has placed a mirror that points out of his office window. However, the mirror is hidden behind a curtain, safe from others' eyes and ridicule. Another cure is an arrow-shaped weathervane aiming at the corner.

4. Here the neighboring house is both larger, and an angle points threateningly at the house. Thus the neighbor is in a stronger position

and the occupants of the smaller house will feel overpowered and will eventually fail in their pursuits. When the neighbor's house is taller, it confounds this problem.

CURE. Grow trees along the border of the two properties, or add a spotlight in a corner beamed toward the smaller house. If the neighboring house is taller, install a mirror aiming at the house, or a bamboo flagpole, or arrow whirligig between the two houses.

5. In this arrangement, with two adjacent corners, neighbors will constantly bicker and sue each other.

CURE. Both neighbors should build adjoining sheds or garages to create a harmonious triangle. (See chapter 8 on the Three Harmonies.)

6. Here, residents of both houses will enjoy a safe, stable, and peaceful environment.

7. When a house abuts a factory, residents should beware of its overbearing influence and bad ch'i and pollution.

CURE. Install plants, lamps, or, even better, a fountain along the border.

Businesses

Businesses should also enjoy good external feng shui. Many companies pay premiums for good views, especially those of water. Mirrors are strategically hung to draw in good views and harness good ch'i—and opportunity. On the day a writer had mirrors installed in her office to reflect a river outside, she claims she received unsolicited calls from two different magazines. There are other means to create your own good feng shui. For example, near Los Angeles, a restaurateur installed an artificial spring in front of her home entrance to make her enterprises more profitable. Fountains are one of the most potent uses of water, which symbolizes ch'i circulation and money. When the Singapore Hyatt was suffering from low occupancy, the management turned on a long-dormant fountain, changed the position of the door, and initiated some other feng shui tactics. Before long, because of extensive flight delays, 450 stranded passengers were brought to the hotel, and ever since it has been flourishing at full occupancy. A prime example of the modern application of feng shui is the Bank of China Building in Hong Kong designed by I.M. Pei (see photograph 1). Although the building is auspiciously oriented on a slope facing Hong Kong harbor, the site was too exposed to several active roadways that surrounded it. The architects sought to create a positive environment protected from urban influences. The auspicious and restorative influence of water was incorporated in a sequence of tranquil pools and active waterfalls around the building. Situated amid strands of bamboo and quince which mask traffic disturbances, the seventy-story tower—the largest in Asia—will dominate the harbor. Note an unintentional feng shui by-product of the design: the sloped glass walls both distort the reflections and ward off the impact of nearby buildings.

Drawing in business is an important concern in feng shui. The ideal situation is for a business to be sited on a streetcorner with the entrance on a diagonal, drawing in ch'i, customers, and money from two directions. Though slants are generally undesirable—omens of unexpected calamities or oblique goings-on—there are certain circumstances when they are helpful. In China, gambling houses first used these slanted doors as a means to an illicit end; they provided optimal opportunities to trap gamblers' ch'i and money. In later years, eyebrows were raised in Hong Kong when a reputable Chinese bank used this same type of entrance. In New York, the inner door of the Chinatown branch of Chemical Bank is strangely askew. If a column stands directly in front of the door, slanted doors' positive effects will be blocked.

CURE. If the column is square, hang a mirror on it to help ch'i permeate its obstructiveness, or mix ju-sha in wine and write on the column, "When exiting, receive blessings."

For restaurants or most small businesses, the entrance should be eye-catching enough to attract customer's ch'i. Healthy plants placed alongside an entrance are both indications of good ch'i and attractive signposts beckoning customers (as Professor Lin noted when he visited Le Cirque, a restaurant in New York). Similarly, a moving object, like a revolving barber's pole, will attract clients. In Burlingame, California, Foto-Foto, a video-photography store, enjoyed good business in part because of a series of neon-lighted arrows in the window that symbolized recycled ch'i, and a red brick walkway leading across the sidewalk to its entrance. Within a year, business increased to the extent that a rival video store, three doors away, folded.

Another way to entice business is to hang wind chimes near the entrance. The sound of wind chimes seems more effective than large signs for drawing both attention and patrons. Wind chimes hanging on or near doors also double as alarms, alerting owners to the comings and goings of would-be clients—or robbers. In Philadelphia, the Kress Express, a health-food cafeteria near the University of Pennsylvania, found summer business slow, and customers habitually entered through a small side door instead of the main entrance. After wind chimes were hung by the main door, business improved noticeably. Shortly afterward, the owner sold out for a handsome sum.

Views of anything associated with death are generally avoided, as they connote failure and decline. Churches are considered bad neighbors because they emit malign ch'i from funerals and somber services. Some companies in New York have covered their windows to avoid overlooking St. Patrick's Cathedral. A design importer who lives and works in Olympic Tower, directly above the cathedral, hung a mirror by her window to deflect both the church's disturbing and sorrowful ch'i and the threatening points of its spires.

Similarly, funeral parlors can hurt businesses, as was the case of a restaurant sited next to one in Virginia. Several previous businesses had failed there, until a feng shui expert suggested planting shrubbery outside the windows to block patrons' views of hearses and mourners. No sooner was this done than business picked up.

Siting a business. When siting a business on a street, the merchant must first observe pedestrian traffic to see which side of the street is the most traveled. In feng shui terms, a street has a "mother" side and a "son" side—a crowded and a less crowded side respectively. Further observation will reveal other patterns of the area's ch'i. For example, a popular movie theater in the middle of a block may be a good neighbor for a new store. But the store owner should also discern the most traveled routes to the theater. Certain routes are preferred, even though they may be more circuitous than others. If not situated along such a route, the store might not benefit from its proximity to the theater, because moviegoers may come from a different direction. The preferred route may have better ch'i—such as one passing a bank with a money machine in it. People prefer to walk by it before going to a movie to pick up some cash or absorb money ch'i, even though that route is twice as long as another. Another consideration is the direction of car traffic. See the following illustrations.

1. Store number 1 is well-situated, but is less attractive than store 4, whose door opens to the advantage of traffic flow.

2. The slanted door is good because it attracts people, their money, and good ch'i from two directions. It is also correctly oriented to acquire ch'i from street traffic flow. However, the support column angle points at the door, giving exiting customers an uncomfortable

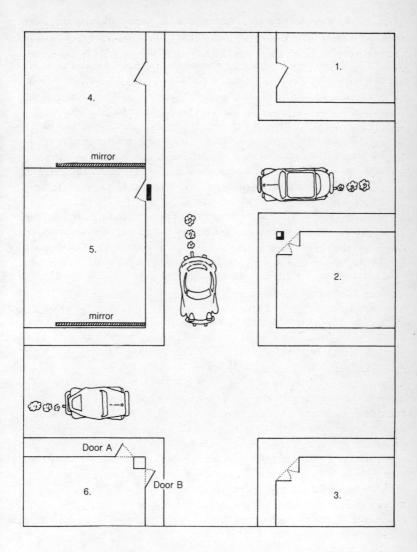

SITING A BUSINESS

feeling, as though their ch'i were blocked. Eventually they will not return.

CURE. Mirror the interior sides of the column.

3. This is the best site for a business, because it grabs ch'i and traffic from all directions.

4. Customers can enter easily; to improve business further, the owner can install a mirror on the wall facing the traffic, thus enlarging the store symbolically and drawing customers' ch'i inside.

5. With a road pointing directly at it, this store will be more stable if the traffic flows away from it. If the traffic flows toward it, the store should be wide with a mirror on the interior wall facing the door. If the store is not wide, hang mirrors on either side of the door to help ward off the oncoming road's ill effect.

6. Here, the column separates two doors, making business uneven. Door A is not beneficial to the store because it does not open to embrace traffic as does door B. Doors for businesses should open inward to encourage the ch'i to flow inside; also, this makes it easier for customers to enter and harder to leave.

———5———

SHAPES

SYING

Shapes can mold our lives. With trained eyes and active imaginations, feng shui experts can identify and interpret the shape of a mountain, a pond, a land plot, a building, or a room, and then discern how it may influence our lives. They apply feng shui techniques to a shape either to enhance or—if the shape has a negative connotation—alter it to create a positive and powerful environment.

Feng shui is a language of symbols. (As we have seen in chapter 4, mountains and rivers are fickle dragons that can guard or threaten residents.) From ancient times to the present, feng shui has been used to interpret natural and man-made signs and shapes—buildings, mountains, plots, rivers, or roads—and divine their effects on us. For example, the Chinese traditionally avoid death-oriented symbolism, ranging from tombstone-shaped buildings to twin towers reminiscent of incense sticks placed on ancestral altars. Even recently, a high-ranking bank officer stationed in Hong Kong found it nearly impossible to sell his charming home in the New Territories because of a coffin-shaped garden in front of the house.

We mirror our surroundings. A home or an office is not merely an inanimate form or an empty shell where we live and work and through which we walk. Its shape takes on meaning that we recognize and react to, both consciously and subconsciously. Moreover, the placement of rooms and furniture within a building determines our habits, reactions, and effectiveness.

The feng shui principles for man-made shapes—ranging from rooms, apartments, and offices to houses and entire buildings—are similar to those applied to plots of land. Square, rectangular, or round shapes generally are best. They are solid, regular shapes from which to build a steady life and fortune. Inner courtyards are desirable, as they help ch'i permeate the house. (The traditional Chinese house was usually an enclave of four single-story buildings arranged to create an interior court—perhaps a geometric reflection of the ideal mountain arrangement.)

The U- and L-shaped houses common in the West, however, have built-in problems. According to feng shui, these shapes are incomplete and occupants will find areas in their life lacking. Therefore, the placement of certain rooms—the master bedroom, the kitchen, and the dining room—becomes particularly important in determining the occupants' destiny.

L-SHAPES

The Chinese avoid L-shaped houses, since they connote something missing or unbalanced. The resulting problems, depending on the rooms involved, can range from minor disruptions, such as children's bad study habits, to major, life-threatening crises. An L-shaped home or office can be resolved on the inside or through landscaping (see chapter 8). The cure for a simple L-shaped house is to install a fountain, tree, or statue, or aim a floodlight at the roof of the house, to symbolically square the L. With L-shaped apartments, obviously a light or tree can't be installed outside, so the imbalance must be corrected in more subtle, interior ways.

CURE. Install a light or hang a wind chime or a crystal ball near the front door to balance the apartment's ch'i, or hang a mirror on a wall aimed at the entrance to reflect the door back on to the correct wall in the following illustration.

With L-shapes, the position of the front door may affect marital stability. A master bedroom, kitchen, or dining room situated in a wing that juts beyond the front door portends potential marital problems. One spouse will tend to sleep or eat away from home, and the family's unity will fall apart.

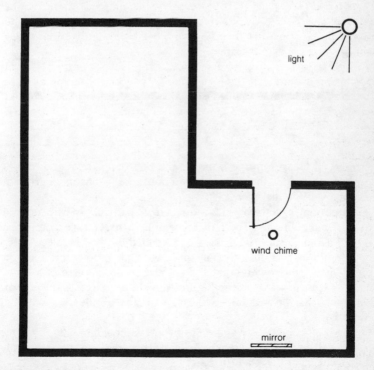

L-SHAPED HOME

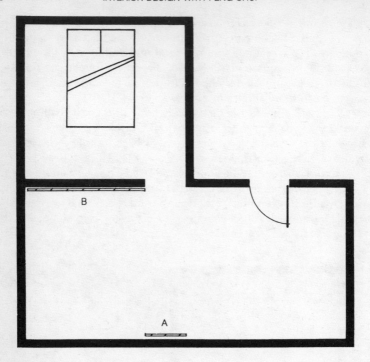

CURE FOR PROTUDING WING

CURE. (A) Hang a mirror opposite the bedroom, kitchen, or dining room door to draw the wing into the house, or (B) hang a mirror on the wall outside the wing.

Boot or cleaver-shaped building's have particularly bad connotations. In a building or a room that resembles a meat cleaver, occupants should avoid placing the desk, stove, or bed on the blade edge. If a building forms a vertical cleaver shape with a high tower, it is advisable to live in the tower—or handle—section. In the case of a house or an apartment—a horizontal knife—it is best to sleep in the narrow wing—the handle—to improve ch'i and give residents a sense of control.

CURE. If a bed, desk, or stove lies on the knife edge, hang a mirror on the wall opposite the edge to bring the bed, desk, or stove symbolically away from the blade to safety.

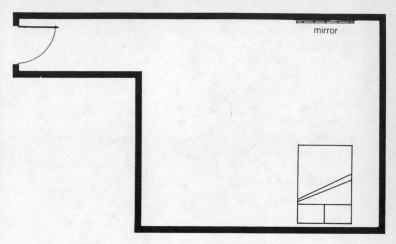

mirror

"CLEAVER" SHAPES

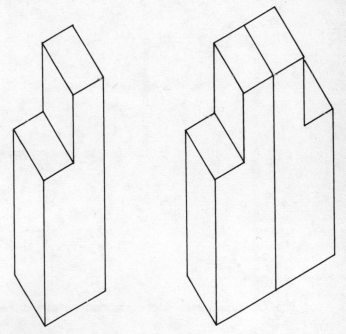

CLEAVER-SHAPED HIGH-RISES

In boot-shaped houses, apartments, or rooms, avoid having the bed, desk, stove, or door in the toe, or you will "trip up" in life. This is especially bad for finances; one can become bankrupt. The ankle area, however, is fortuitous: the joint of power and energy.
CURES.

1. Plant flower beds at point A, then link them to the top of the boot with vines. This will tip the toe up from the heavier side, thus removing pressure.

2. Install a pool or a lamp at point B to symbolically make the shape a complete square or rectangle.

3. Hang a mirror to reflect the bed, desk, stove, or door away from the sole of the boot.

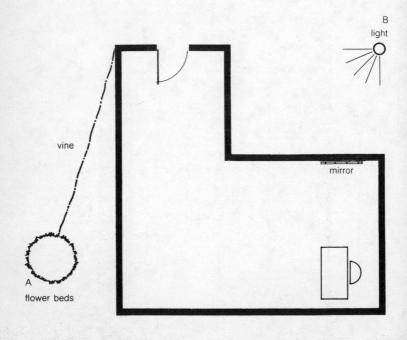

"BOOT" SHAPES

Many American homes are designed with the garage jutting out from the main section of the house—again creating an L. The protruding garage obstructs the exit route so that those exiting or entering must continually walk around it. Even though a path leads from the door to the garage, the entrance will feel blocked, hindering career growth. A path leading in the opposite direction offers an alternative route that widens career possibilities and balances residents' ch'i.

When a garage creates an L and obstructs the route leading from the front door, it is unbalancing to occupants' bodies and minds. For example, in the accompanying illustration, they will always think "right," and aim for the garage, so the residents' future will be narrow and sidetracked.

CURES.

1. Install a floodlight aimed at the door to even out the shape.

2. Build a rock, brick, or cement pathway leading from the door to another roadway to balance the house's exit and to open a new road, creating and widening opportunities.

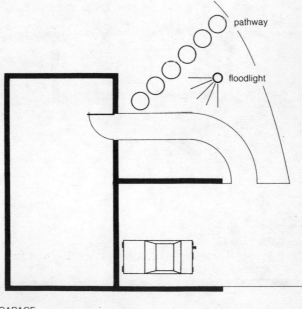

L-SHAPE: GARAGE

U-SHAPES

U-shaped houses and apartments with the entrance inside the U can be unlucky for marriages. Avoid placing the master bedroom, kitchen, or dining area in the wings, or a spouse will frequently eat or sleep out. Symbolically "locked out" of the house, they will stay out a lot and eventually not even come home. In addition, the family may be plagued with chronic headaches, surgery, or business and job losses.
CURES.

1. Relocate a guest room rather than a principal room in a wing of the U.

2. With a house, plant a line of flowers or shrubs from one wing to another to even out the shape, forming a rectangle.

3. In an apartment, hang mirrors to reflect the projecting room inside the main part of the house.

4. Hang a mirror on the wall outside the wing—if it is a bedroom, dining area, or kitchen—facing into the house.

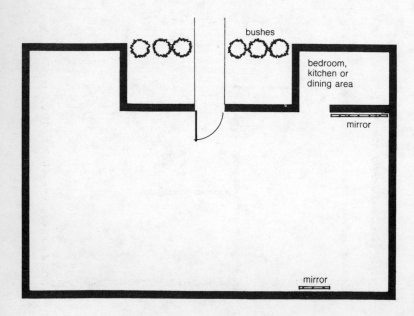

U-SHAPE: CURVES

IRREGULAR SHAPES

As with land and plot shapes, one can use the balancing method to reinterpret irregularly shaped buildings, apartments, and rooms. For example, a house with a small entrance—a "nose"—admits only an inadequate amount of ch'i, so finances will be choked, and residents' health will suffer. Plants can resolve this imbalance.

In a pointed house or one with sharp angles—which threaten occupants—unsuspected accidents may befall residents.
CURE. If coupled with a balancing pool, fountain, or plants, the house will acquire a harmonious feeling of balanced yin and yang. (See illustration on p. 74.)

Odd- or irregularly shaped houses can be lucky if properly supplemented. In California, a young family moved into a windmill-shaped house. For people with very slow ch'i, this shape might enliven them. But it was too dynamic and contorted for the new occupants, making the wife suffer from intestinal problems and headaches.
CURE. To stabilize the home, tie the house's windmill shape down at each corner by planting vines.

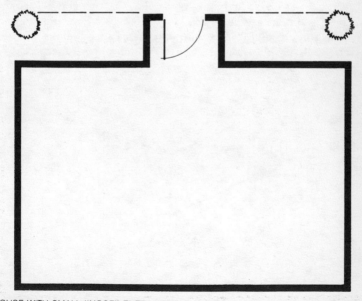

HOUSE WITH SMALL "NOSE" ENTRANCE

Plant bushes or flowers to complete the shape.

VARIOUS HOUSE SHAPES

1.–3. Regular shapes in the illustrations are best. House Number 3 can be further improved by planting bushes to create an octagon. Irregular shapes are more risky: some can be auspicious, while others can portend problems. However, even the most troublesome shapes can be cured, usually by referring to the ba-gua (see chapter 8).

4.–5. These are lucky shapes.

6. This shape will be good for residents' marriage, finances, scholarship, and patronage.

7. This shape is good; the best places for bedrooms are in corners A and B.

8. This shape is also good. If the entrance is on side A, residents' careers will prosper; on side B, children will thrive; on side C, occupants will enjoy renown; and on side D, the family will be harmonious. This shape, however, can be improved. The addition of wings (A and B) will make the shape luckier.

9. Residents of a house built in this shape will enjoy much wealth and a good marriage.

10. A stairlike or lightning-bolt house shape is good. The more stairlike additions are built, the better. This is where intuition and imagination are useful in adding extensions to buildings to create symbolically powerful shapes. One feng shui expert interpreted the

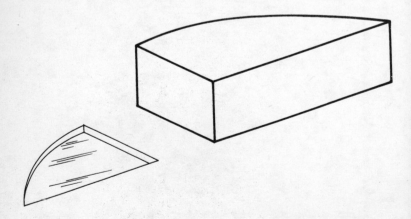

IRREGULARLY SHAPED CURVE

This unusually shaped house was enhanced and made whole by a balancing pool.

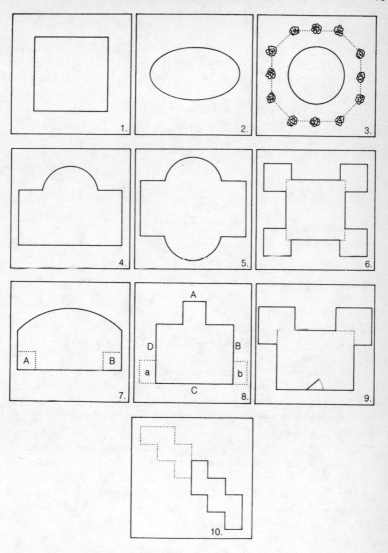

HOUSE SHAPES

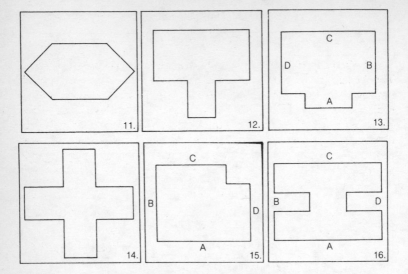

shape as a powerful lightning bolt—a design used by a major computer company to improve business.

11. Although this shape is generally auspicious, avoid having doors on the slanted sides, or unexpected calamities may occur.

12. A T-shaped house is generally good if the shaft of the T is not too long—longer than the width of the crossbar. The best area to site the bedroom is in the stem and not on the ends of the crossbar.

13. Residents of this house will have a number of shortcomings. If the entrance is on side A, they will lack scholarship and patronage; on side B, wealth and scholarship will be lacking; on side C, they will have marriage and wealth woes; on side D, they will have marital and patronage problems.

14. A cross is very unfortunate. Residents will suffer in marital, financial, scholarship, and patronage areas. This shape is called an "injured dragon," and occupants can expect to lose property.

15. This shape suffers the same shortcomings as more pronounced L shapes. If the entrance is on side A, occupants' marriage will suffer; on side B, money problems will result; on side C, poor scholarship; on side D, lack of patronage.
CURE. Plant a tree or install a light at the "missing" corner.

16. H shapes are unlucky, and the deeper the hollows, the worse the situation will be. If the entrance is on sides A or C, residents will have family and offspring trouble, and on sides B and D, career and reputation complications.
CURE. Square off the shape with plants or paths.

VARIOUS ROOM SHAPES

1.–9. These numbers in the illustration are good, whole shapes. The hexagram of number 2 is a lucky shape and can be further improved if either plants or a group of six colored objects—white, red, yellow, green, blue, and black—are placed in each corner. (Six colors represent the Buddhist's Six True Words; see Appendix 1.) If number 4 is a bedroom, place the bed on the wall opposite the protruding section, then install a plant, crystal ball, or light in the protrusion.

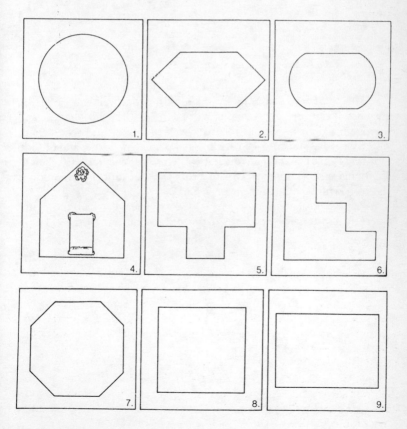

ROOM SHAPES

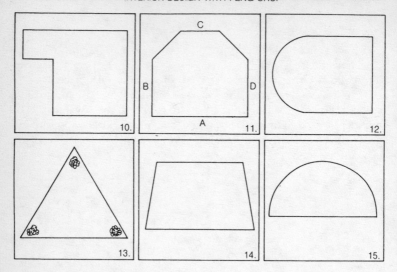

10.–15. These are unlucky shapes. In room number 11, if the entrance is on side A, occupants will have trouble with finances and marriage; a door on side B means a lack of money and scholarship; a door on side C means lack of scholarship and patronage; and on side D it brings marital and patronage problems (see chapter 8). Triangular rooms such as number 13 can bring disaster unless each angle is resolved with a round object or a plant.

Rhomboid-shaped rooms, such as number 14, can cause unforeseen disasters for residents if the door is on one of the slanting walls.

6

INTERIORS: ELEMENTS OF STRUCTURE

STRUCTURE

In modern-day life, interior feng shui seems to affect us more than exterior considerations such as mountains and rivers. Both office arrangement and the home base influence our behavior in the outside world—yin affects yang. A person's behavior patterns and life course can be determined simply by the structure, shape, and furniture arrangement of the rooms he or she inhabits.

Seeking positive, healthy ch'i, the feng shui expert examines the home or offices as if it were a body with its own metabolism. Doors and windows are the mouths and eyes letting the correct amount of ch'i enter into a home. Halls are veins and arteries conducting ch'i from room to room. And furniture, plants, and inner doors channel ch'i throughout the rooms. Even the most appealing and impressive interior may harbor the germs of problems that only the trained eye of a feng shui expert can spot.

A house or an office may look beautiful and comfortable, with good views and the stamp of a well-known designer or architect. But, according to Lin Yun, such an arrangement, like the one illustrated, can be riddled with feng shui defects. The division into two halves may cause sickness along the central line of the inhabitant's body.

In the illustration—an award-winning home built in California—some feng shui alterations help prevent the built-in problems.

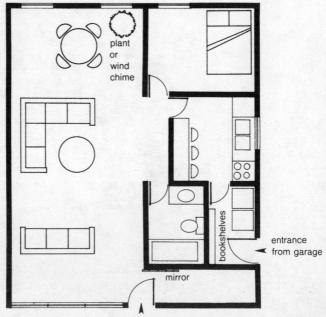

A PROBLEMATIC HOME

One of the main drawbacks is the unbalanced entrance. The door opens to present a long-distance view partially disrupted by a wall, which unbalances the residents' immediate perception on entering and will eventually affect both work and marriage. Every day when they return home the right eye sees the corner of the wall and the left eye sees the distant view, disrupting their ch'i and affecting ·both language and motion. The divided view will hurt the "speech" side of the brain while it develops the "movement" side—causing the occupants to think less and act more. Invariably, couples will quarrel instead of discussing problems, and ultimately resort to violence.

CURE. Place a mirror, a picture, or flowers on the wall to attract the right eye and to create a more harmonious effect. (Lin Yun recommends nine dollar bills for businessmen.)

The home's door-window alignment funnels ch'i too quickly from one side of the house out the other, threatening—like a knife— residents' health and forming an invisible barrier that can harm family relationships. The fast-flowing ch'i also carries away money and opportunity.

CURE. Hang a plant or a wind chime to disperse ch'i evenly throughout the house.

Once the entrance is resolved, residents may still encounter pitfalls. For example, though the main part of the house is spacious and well designed, its positive qualities may be of little help if residents choose to enter through the garage and immediately face a wall. Also, since the door opens the wrong way, they will have to walk around it, then brush against the washing machine, navigate a sequence of sharp corners, oppressively high bookshelves, constrained hallways, and other obstacles. Such a contorted pathway to the bedroom will unbalance the occupants' ch'i. Eventually they will suffer from lethargy—a tendency to collapse in the bed when they return home—bad humor, and marital and familial discord.

DOORS

In an ideal house, apartment, or office, the flow of ch'i should be smooth, similar to the circulation in a healthy body. Exterior doors and windows are orifices allowing ch'i and opportunities to enter. Ideally, interior doors, hallways, and stairs pump ch'i evenly throughout the house. The circulation should be smooth, not too quick and not too slow.

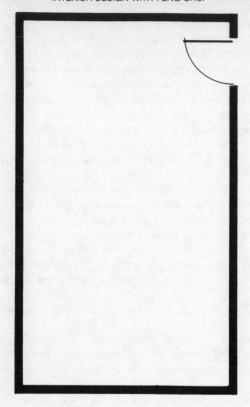

IDEAL
ENTRANCE

Entrance doors should open to the widest area of the room or foyer. The foyer—the occupant's first impression of a home or an office and the opening for ch'i—is a crucial feng shui consideration. An entrance area should be light and expansive, warm and welcoming. This encourages residents' ch'i to rise and flow smoothly.

In Washington, D.C., Johnny Kao, owner of a number of Chinese restaurants, had an expert draw up the floor plan for Mr. K's, a large restaurant he opened in 1983. Among other changes, he installed a *trompe l'oeil* tapestry of the Temple of Heaven on the wall facing the entrance. He said it made both symbolic and design sense. "This temple itself is where the emperor annually prayed for a good year and harvest for China," he explained, adding that "the three-dimensional quality creates a vista, so customers are not greeted by a blank wall."

Here are a number of problems and cures to deal with the potential structural inadequacies of a house.

A door that opens the wrong way into a wall will cramp occupants' ch'i and luck. Eventually they will also suffer from physical problems and emotional anxiety.

CURE. Change the hinges so that the door opens the other way, hang a mirror on the wall to create an illusion of greater space, or install a light or bell that goes on or rings automatically when the door is opened.

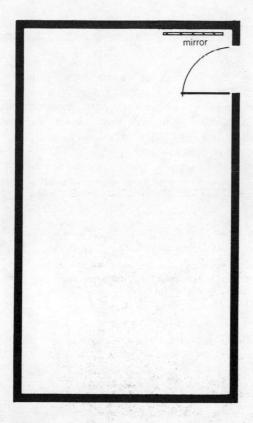

CRAMPED ENTRANCE

"BRICK WALL" ENTRANCE

If a person returns home every day to be greeted by a wall, it will become a literal "brick wall," inhibiting ch'i and guaranteeing a life of struggle—if not failure within three years, according to Lin Yun. CURE. Hang a mirror on the wall to allow ch'i to penetrate the oppressive space.

A constrained or dark entrance oppresses ch'i, choking residents' luck. If the entrance is a narrow hallway, it can cause health problems ranging from respiratory ailments to difficult and dangerous births. Psychologically, a narrow, poorly lit entrance is depressing, leading to morose and melancholy moods.
CURE. Install a bright ceiling light and a mirror on the wall to create depth.

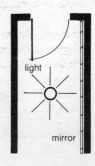

NARROW ENTRANCE

Back doors are also important, as they represent indirect opportunities. A home or a business would do better with a back door opening out to a wide path, symbolizing greater chances of financial growth, than to a restrictive wall.

Door Alignment

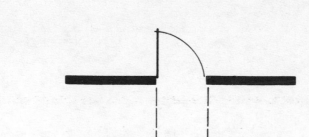

GOOD DOOR ALIGNMENT

Door alignment is important in feng shui. Awkwardly placed doors can cause health problems and personality conflicts. Doors aligned directly opposite each other are usually fine, as are doors that don't overlap. However, avoid having two bathroom doors face each other. Occupants may fall sick along the central line of their bodies or they may suffer from physical and financial diarrhea, with health or money running out.

CURE. Hang mirrors on both doors facing the hall.

If the entrance is directly opposite the back door, good ch'i enters and leaves too quickly to circulate. As a result, residents may have many opportunities come their way, but they will not be able to hold on to and take advantage of them. The closer together these doors, the worse the situation. The farther apart, the better, providing a greater chance for ch'i to circulate.

CURE. Hang a wind chime, plant, or crystal ball to disperse ch'i and thus spread opportunity through the house. The entrance of a foundering building contractor's home in Tucson, Arizona, led straight to the door to the garden. After hanging a wind chime to encourage circulation of ch'i—and opportunities—he landed a huge project that led to more money and more referrals.

Doorknobs that knock together like gnashing teeth can create family conflicts.

CURE. To remedy this quarrelsome door arrangement, either paint a red dot at eye level on the offending doors or perform a healing ritual as follows. Tie an 18- or 27-inch red ribbon on each knob, then cut the ribbon in half (see Appendix 1).

Beware of opposite doors that appear aligned but are actually slightly askew. They can cause health, career, and family problems. As insidious as a "bad bite," this dangerous arrangement will ensure that family members are at odds. The "knifelike" corner of each door-frame can subtly unbalance residents' ch'i.

CURE. Hang an ornament at eye level on the doorframe that juts into one's view.

1. Even worse than the "bad bite" doors are two obviously overlapping parallel doors. This misalignment can be harmful to health and to personal and office relationships by creating an uneven vista that will unbalance ch'i. It is like having one far-sighted eye and one near-sighted eye. One side of the resident may feel expansive while the other side will feel constrained, so the body and the emotions will be unbalanced.

CURE. Hang a mirror or a picture on the overlapping wall to create the illusion of expanded space, thus harmonizing the occupants' ch'i and allowing them to have a more balanced body and focused perspective. This will also divert the residents' attention away from the cutting edge of the doorframe. The picture can be of an attractive view, a child, or—for a would-be aggressive businessman—an actual hundred-dollar bill.

BAD DOOR ALIGNMENTS

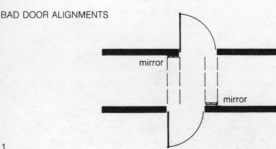

1.

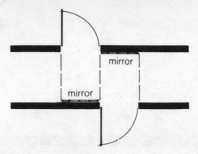

2.

2. These doors can be inhibiting to residents. Pictures with vistas or mirrors hung opposite the doors will correct the misalignment.

3. If one parallel door is larger than its opposite, it can be good or bad, depending on the circumstances. It is fine if the larger door opens into a large room—a bedroom or a living room—and the smaller door leads to a closet or a bathroom. But if the larger door leads to a bathroom, a kitchen, or a closet, and the smaller door opens into a bedroom, this is bad because, as a Chinese saying goes, "Big eats little." The ch'i of the kitchen, bathroom, or closet will overwhelm the bedroom ch'i; thus the resident will be drawn to lesser activities. For example, a larger door leading to a bathroom may waste the resident's time and cause health (usually abdominal) problems. The occupants may suffer from intestinal or bladder complications or become preoccupied with preparing to go out—such as applying makeup—instead of actually going out. If the larger door opens to a closet, residents will likely be vain and spend an inordinate amount of time dressing up. If the larger door opens to the kitchen, residents will be obsessed with food, cooking, and eating.
CURE. Hang a mirror on the larger door to reflect the bedroom into it, so both doors seem to lead to bedrooms.

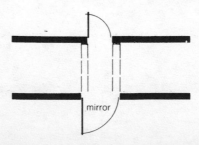

3.

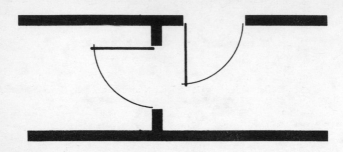

4. AWKWARDLY PLACED DOORS

4. Avoid awkwardly placed doors. In a three-bedroom Park Avenue apartment in New York, a door that opened to partially block another doorway caused the owner's son to break his collar bone navigating around it. This hazard was cleared up by replacing the first door with smaller louvered doors.

5. For family or office harmony, another situation to avoid is a small hallway with many doors. Each door represents a different "mouth" with its own opinion. To stop residents from continually bickering, hang mirrors on the doors or install a bright light or a wind chime overhead.

6. A door situated at the end of a long hallway endangers residents' health; again, intestinal problems may arise from fast ch'i flow, which ricochets off the wall, giving residents an explosive feeling,

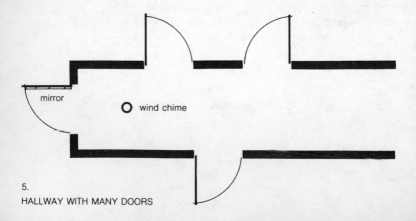

mirror

wind chime

5.
HALLWAY WITH MANY DOORS

6.
DOOR AT END OF LONG HALLWAY

affecting their nerves and their digestion, and making them easy to upset. A door or a wall at the end of the hallway also creates a dead end that may block chances of developing a career.

CURE. Hang a mirror on the door or wall to deflect strong ch'i flow and to create a longer vista so that symbolically residents have hope for advancement. Without a mirror, they would have no place to go. Hallways should not be cluttered, presenting a stumbling block to ch'i and the residents' future.

Traditionally, the Chinese avoid three or more doors or windows in a row. (Windows are relatively less problematic than doors.) The superstitious explanation is that demons or malign ch'i fly in straight lines, so screens were used to deflect their evil influence. Basically, this door-window lineup creates a draft and funnels ch'i too quickly. It inhibits occupants' ch'i, harming their health, personal relations, and inner harmony. Occupants may fall ill along the central meridians of their bodies; generally this means intestinal problems. The fast flow of ch'i can also serve as an invisible barrier, causing strained relations at home or in the office. To stop ch'i from flowing too quickly, hang a wind chime or crystal ball to disperse ch'i.

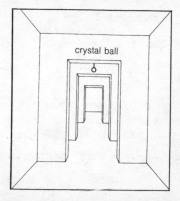

THREE OR MORE DOORS OR WINDOWS IN A ROW

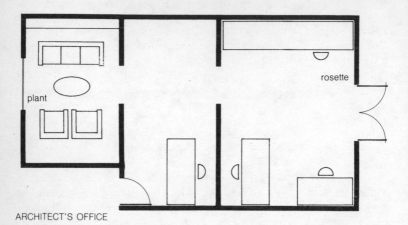

ARCHITECT'S OFFICE

A Philadelphia architect was surprised when a feng shui expert visiting his office cited a series of doors and windows to intuit a rift with his partner, and observed that good prospects continuously eluded them. The strongly funneled ch'i divided their desks and carried away opportunities. In addition, said the architect, the misalignment of the doors caused a further strain and tension in the office, and business was foundering. After he hung a plant in the window and installed an ornamental rosette on the wall next to a door leading to a garden, relations thawed and business picked up substantially. Wind chimes, beaded curtains, and crystal balls are also effective dispersers of fast-flowing ch'i.

Door size is important. A door should be in proportion to house or room size. A relatively small door will operate as if it were a small mouth or windpipe; it will not allow enough good ch'i to enter and circulate, thus diminishing residents' chances of health, wealth, and happiness.

CURE. Hang a mirror above or on both sides of the door to give an effect of greater height or width.

If a door is too large for a house or room, too much ch'i will enter and overwhelm the occupants. Whenever wealth or luck enters—no matter how much—the house will not be able to hold on to it and accumulate savings.

CURE. Paint the foyer a deep color: black, dark blue or green, brown, purple, etc. Or install a heavy object at the entrance, near but not too close to the door.

The ratio of doors to windows is also a feng shui consideration, since it affects family dynamics. Doors represent parents' mouths. Windows are the children's voices. If windows outnumber doors by a three-to-one ratio, there will be arguing caused by too many differing opinions. Children will be insubordinate and talk back. Similarly, if the windows are larger than the door, children will have their way and ignore their parents' guidance, feelings, and discipline. A larger window with small panes is fine.

CURE. To create family harmony, hang a bell or a wind chime near the door so that when it opens, its parental voice will be heard by the windows.

WINDOWS

Windows are the eyes—and mouths—of a home or office. (A broken windowpane may augur eye problems.) As conductors of ch'i, windows should open completely—inwardly or outwardly—instead of sliding up or down. Most admirable is an outward-opening window that allows maximum ch'i to enter and circulate, enhancing residents' ch'i and career opportunities. The outward movement of opening is a harmonious positive action, stretching occupants' ch'i outward. Inward-opening windows encourage timidity, harming residents' ch'i.

Windows that slide up and down, never opening more than halfway, only let in half as much ch'i as their size, and occupants tend to give people a false impression.

Though different climates and geographical locations have their specific needs, as a rule a western-facing window can harm occupants' ch'i. Western sun glare can be intensely oppressive, causing headaches, irrational tempers, and inefficient work. In Hong Kong, many companies black out or even board up their western windows, especially in the afternoons. Better yet, a crystal ball could also be hung to transform the malign sunlight into a rainbow of colors, enhancing the entire room with a ch'i vitalizing force.

The top of a window should be higher than the tallest resident, or it will lower or depress his or her ch'i. Windows also should be relatively wide. Slitlike windows suppress ch'i flow and narrow residents' perspectives and opportunities.

SLANTS

Slanting beams, halls, walls, or doors portend unexpected, oblique, and strange happenings or accidents. This sudden change of affairs could verge on disaster. A cash register under a stairwell is especially bad for business, since the downward slant will draw business away.

CURE. There are several small cures to tip the balance back to normal, or even in your favor. For a slanted beam or ceiling, hang a red tassel, curtain, or wood beam to even out the slant or build a complementary slant.

A door in a slanted wall is particularly bad, especially if it leads to a bedroom or bathroom. Residents will fall victim to strange, unexpected illnesses or events. To prevent a calamity, hang a crystal ball on either side of the door, about a yard from the doorway. For a slanted hall, hang three crystal balls along its entire length.

If an entire wall of a room is slanted, ch'i flow will be trapped in a smaller-than-90-degree angle.

CURE. Place a light or plant in the acute angle to help ch'i circulate.

STAIRS

Stairs are important considerations in feng shui. Conducting ch'i from floor to floor, a staircase should be wide, well-lit, and unconstrained by a low ceiling. If it is dark and narrow, ch'i will be choked; hang a mirror on the ceiling and increase lighting to improve ch'i flow. Avoid stairs with spaces instead of risers between the treads. With this type of stair, ch'i escapes and does not rise upstairs.

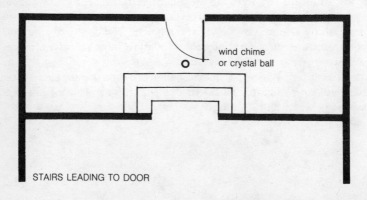

wind chime or crystal ball

STAIRS LEADING TO DOOR

CURE. Install potted plants underneath the stairs to help ch'i circulate from ground level upward to the top. If a stair ends too close to a wall it faces, hang a mirror on the wall to symbolically extend the vista.

The Chinese avoid a stairway that runs straight toward the main door, allowing ch'i and money to roll away.

CURE. Hang a wind chime or a crystal ball between the last stair and the entrance to modify ch'i flow.

If a house is split-level, the owner will have many ups and downs. Life, emotions, and business will be uneven and fraught with difficulties. Flat or duplex homes are best. Split-level steps follow stairway rules—the wider the better, giving residents a safer, more stable feeling.

If a room is split-level, the bed should be on the upper level, but not too cramped. Since more than one step from one level to another endangers residents' health and career, it is best to have wide steps flanked with plants.

A curved, graceful stairway is best. But a spiral staircase is dangerous, boring through floors like a lethal corkscrew. Not only do most spiral stairways lack risers, allowing ch'i to escape, but they are also like holes in the house's body. If the staircase is near the central part of the house, residents may suffer heart or other medical problems within a couple of years (see chapter 8).

CURE. Wrap something green, such as a vine, on the handle or banister. Then install a light on the ceiling above the stairway to shine from the top floor to the bottom.

CEILINGS

Ceilings should be graciously high and well-lit. A low ceiling in a confined space will debilitate residents' ch'i, making them depressed and prone to headaches.

CURE. Install mirrors on the walls on either side to give a more expansive feeling. Auntie Yuan, a successful New York restaurant, resolved an uneven ceiling by painting it black so that its irregularities are less evident, and business thrives. (Black is also a money-inducing color; see chapter 8.)

BEAMS

While some Western homes purposely have exposed joists or rafters to create a rustic mood, beams in a Chinese home are thought to be oppressive structural formations that harm ch'i flow and occupants' luck. As load-bearing beams actually create compression, they can be oppressive to those working, eating, or sleeping underneath, causing health and emotional problems.

Beams in a bedroom can cause various problems, depending on where they are. For example, a beam over the head of a bed can be the source of headaches or migraines, over the stomach area it can cause ulcers and intestinal problems, and over the foot of the bed it may limit the sleeper's mobility geographically and in life. A Florida businessman found he seldom traveled after he began sleeping in a bed where the foot was under a beam.

Beams over the stove or dining area insure financial losses; in particular, lent money will not be returned.

Beams over a workspace can be debilitating. One architect with a creativity block found he worked better once he moved his drafting table out from under a guillotine-like beam.

If the bed, desk, or stove cannot be moved out from under a beam, a symbolic "cure" can resolve the oppressive qualities of the beam and encourage ch'i to penetrate below it. Hang two bamboo flutes with red ribbons wrapped around them to create a ba-gua formation with the beam, thus imitating the auspicious octagon of the *I Ching.* Another method is to attach a red fringe running the length of the beam.

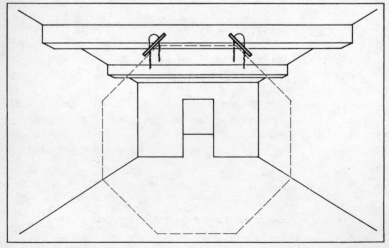

FLUTES AND BEAM

In New York, a beam over a couple's bed seemed to divide them: the wife could not sleep there and would get up in the middle of the night and sleep elsewhere. After flutes were hung to symbolically penetrate the beam's oppressiveness, both spouses slept through the night (see photograph 3).

A beam in a confined area, such as a hallway, can trap good ch'i and thus interfere with its circulation through the house.
CURE. Install bright overhead lights covered by a false ceiling of translucent glass, which not only allows ch'i to flow smoothly but also lifts up the occupants' ch'i.

A narrow hall in New York was plagued with five doors—which caused family fights, and two beams—which obstructed ch'i flow. A false "shoji screen" ceiling lit by warm fluorescent lights smoothed both ch'i circulation and family relations (see photographs 2A, 2B).

CORNERS

Projecting corners are considered unfortunate structures. They are similar to sharp knives or accusing fingers pointing at occupants, threatening and harming them and undercutting their ch'i. For example, residents may be in for a mugging or undeserved criticism.
CURE. To resolve such a corner, either hang a mirror on one or both sides to soften the edge, grow a vine up the edge to camouflage it, or hang a crystal ball in front of it.

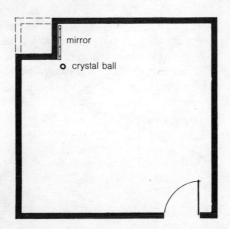

PROJECTING CORNER

COLUMNS

Interior columns play a part in feng shui. Rounded ones are better than square, as they allow ch'i to flow smoothly around them. Besides obstructing ch'i, square columns have sharp angles that point in a threatening way at occupants.

CURE. Install mirrors on all sides of the column to encourage ch'i flow (make sure they run from edge to edge), or hang vines on each corner to soften the edges. After one United Nations employee installed mirrors on a large column in her office, she received numerous promotions, much freedom in her work, and many prestigious titles. "Others around me work hard, but go nowhere," she said. "I work less hard and am very successful and get to represent my department at various conferences around the world."

ROOM ARRANGEMENT

The placement of rooms within a home can affect residents' behavior. Besides influencing residents' ch'i, the layout creates a pattern of activity and gradually dictates how they pass their time and think. For instance, the room nearest the entrance will, by the suggestive nature of its use and contents, determine residents' life-style at home—especially if it is located very close to the main door.

When analyzing a house's layout, feng shui experts pay much attention to the placement of the master bedroom, kitchen, and front entrance—or garage entrance. This is because we spend a third of our lives in the bedroom, so its impact on us is substantial. The kitchen is the household's access and approach to money. The entrance is our first impression of home and the opening of ch'i.

1.–2. Studies, living rooms, and foyers are the most desirable rooms to have near the entrance. If the first sight upon entering is a living room, the residents will relax and make themselves at home. If the first sight is a study, residents will tend to be bookish, caught up in work, studies, or letter-writing.

3. If the first room is a kitchen, however, the household will be food oriented. The sight of the kitchen will create a Pavlovian need for food, encouraging excessive eating. Children are most vulnerable, and are liable to grow fat. They will be scolded often because their studies will suffer while they eat compulsively. In addition, the proximity of the kitchen to the entrance increases the tendency that visitors will come only to eat. A New York artist, on the advice of a feng shui

expert, painted a screen that greeted her guests and shielded their eyes from the kitchen and dining table. She happily found her guests paying more attention to her art and less to her cooking.

4. If the first room one sees when entering a home is a bathroom, the residents' health and wealth will suffer—money will get flushed away. The occupants will spend a great deal of time there, either primping and washing their hands or dealing with bladder problems. When they return home, they will feel the urge to enter the bathroom before they put the key in the lock.

5. If a bedroom is the first sight when one enters, residents will habitually be tired and in need of rest when they return home.

6. With a game room directly in front of the entrance, occupants will fritter away their time and money at games.

CURE FOR NUMBERS 3–6. Hang a mirror on the outside of the room's door, or a beaded curtain or a wind chime if there is no door.

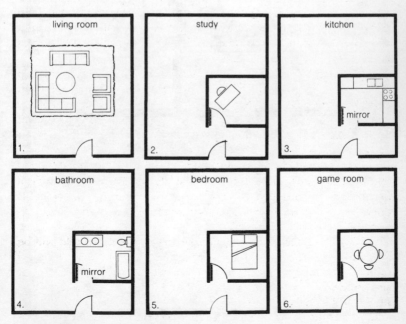

ROOM PLACEMENT: FIRST IMPRESSIONS

A master bedroom should be behind the central meridian of the house. Ideally, it should be sited catercorner to the entrance door for maximum control over one's destiny. The closer the bedroom is to the front door, the less peace residents will feel. If the room is far from the entrance, the bed will be more separate from the outside world, so residents can sleep better and feel more secure and peaceful. If the entrance is situated on the side of the house and does not face the road, site the bedroom according to the entrance; if possible, have the bedroom in the area farthest from both the entrance and the road. CURE. Hang a mirror behind the central meridian, facing the bedroom, to symbolically draw the room away from the front part of the home.

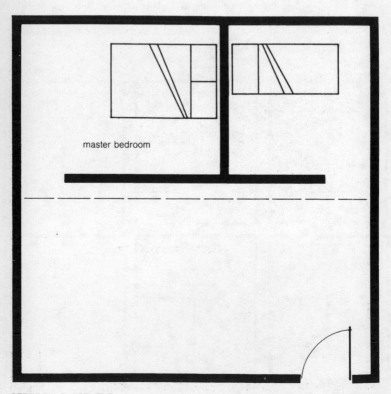

master bedroom

BEDROOM PLACEMENT

Bathrooms and the kitchen should not be located on the central line of the house or residents will be ill somewhere along the central line of their bodies. If the bathroom is in the center, luck will peter out and money will be flushed away. It is fine if the kitchen is on the center line and is wide and roomy, with good ventilation; residents will have room to move and advance in life and finances. If the kitchen is narrow or if an oven or microwave is on the top of the range and oppresses it, however, the cook will be peevish and family fortunes will dwindle.

CURE. If the kitchen is narrow, hang a mirror behind the stove to symbolically increase the number of burners and the amount of food (symbolizing money) made. Also, hang mirrors on doors facing the outside of the room, reflecting the kitchen away from the center. A wind chime should be hung above the chef's station.

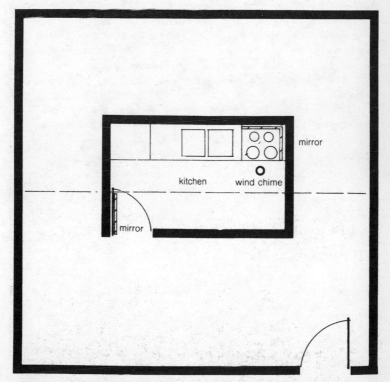

KITCHEN OR BATHROOM PLACEMENT

If a bathroom sits on the central line, hang a full-length mirror on the outside of the bathroom door.

Relative room positioning also has an effect on residents. For example, the kitchen should be as close as possible to the dining room.

A bathroom, the place where water (money) escapes, is a symbol of family members' internal plumbing and expenses, so its position within a home is crucial. Bathrooms should not face the kitchen (food symbolizes wealth) or earned money will be flushed away, and health and finances will suffer.

A bedroom facing a bathroom will also have a bad effect on health, especially along the digestive tract.

CURE. Hang a mirror on the outside of the bathroom door or a crystal ball in the path between the bath and bed.

Avoid having a toilet upstairs from the bedroom.

CURE. Tie a red string from the spot on the ceiling directly under the toilet, run the string along the nearest wall, and attach it to the floor under the bed. Another cure is to mirror the ceiling.

A bathroom should not sit at the end of a long corridor. The hallway will funnel arrowlike ch'i through the bathroom door, harming family members' intestinal or reproductive systems.

CURE. Hang a curtain, wind chime, or mobile in the hallway to disperse ch'i.

The worst place for a toilet is in the center of the house, which, according to Black Hat feng shui, symbolizes the wholeness of the universe—the tai-chi, the center of the *I Ching* octagon.

CURE. Mirror all four interior walls of the bathroom.

1. *The Bank of China Building in Hong Kong designed by I.M. Pei and Partners with a floor plan (see p. 60).*

2A. *Before: Hallway with disruptive beam (right).*
2B. *After: Hallway with enlivening overhead lighting* (see p. 95).

3. *Bamboo flutes in a ba-gua shape remedy a divisive and oppressive beam (left)* (see p. 95).

4. *A well-arranged living room. Bamboo flutes make a ba-gua shape to augment the wealth and marriage areas, mirrors double the space* (see p. 138).

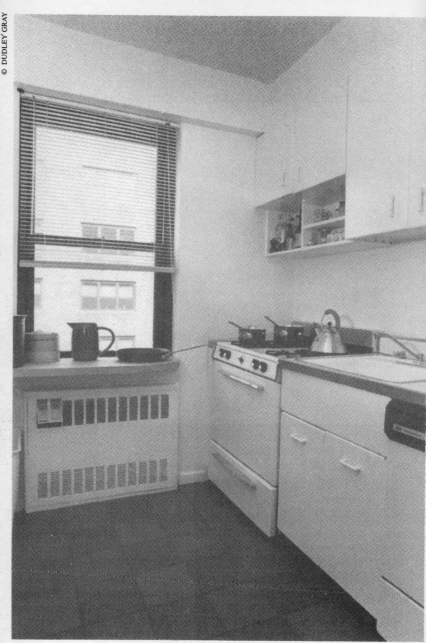

5A. Before: A kitchen without mirrors.

© DUDLEY GRAY

5B. *After* Good use of mirrors in a kitchen (see p. 106).

6. *A skylight invigorates ch'i in this entrance hall. Note the inviting mirror and a plant obscuring an obstructive pillar (above)* (see p. 144).

7A. *Before: A bathroom without mirrors (opposite top)* (see p. 111).

7B. *After: Mirrors enliven and widen a bathroom. Toilet is well out of view upon entering (opposite bottom)* (see p. 111).

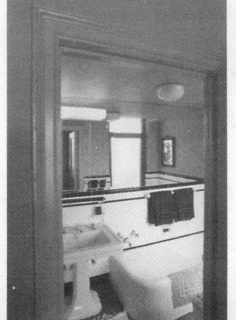

8A. *Furniture arranged in the auspicious octagon of the ba-gua (far left) (see p. 110).*

8B. *Note mirrors on recessed windows that bring in light and city views (left) (see p. 110).*

9. *Feng shui works for any style and taste. A well-placed mirror, plants in front of the fireplqace, and a comfortable furniture arrangement add to the appeal of this living room (below) (see p. 110).*

Room courtesy of Patty Hambrecht.t.

© DUDLEY GRAY

10. *A living room with floor-to-ceiling mirrors has many benefits* *(see p. 110).*

© DUDLEY GRAY

11. *A mirror draws water views (symbolizing money) over a well-placed bed.*

12. *A dining room with a mirrored wall and an auspiciously shaped octagon dining table (see p. 108).*

13. Framed by wood to look like a door, the mirror resolves a slanted wall and reflects anyone entering the real door (see p. 136).

14. *In this study the desk is well-placed facing the door, mirrors bring in views, and a plant is trained up a protruding corner (see p. 115).*

15. *A well-placed office desk (see p. 122).*

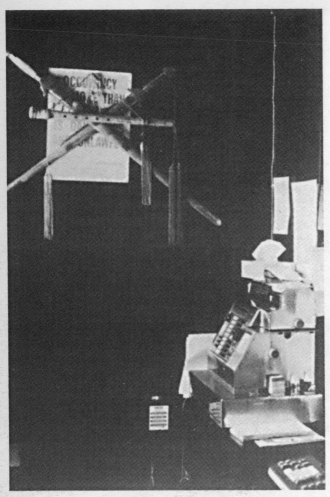

16A. Specially augmented cash register (above) (see p. 124).
16B. Specially augmented bar (right) (see p. 123).

16C. *The welcoming entrance to a New York restaurant, Aunti Yuan. Black walls (the color of water / money) are enlivened by specially blessed calligraphy, such as the word Tao to the left of the desk (see pages 112 and 1237).*

7

FURNITURE PLACEMENT

INTERIOR DECORATION

Along with room structure, furniture placement channels interior ch'i and can thus enhance residents' luck and lives. While feng shui deals with all types of "furniture"—ranging from microwaves and cash registers to bureaus and dining tables—placement of stoves, desks, and beds generally has the greatest impact on people. Their placement can decide whether a person succeeds or not.

HOMES

Bedroom

Our bedroom particularly affects us. It is where we rest, relax, and regain our strength, and the position of the bed is important. Ideally, a bed should lie catercorner to the door so that the occupant has the widest possible view and can see anyone who enters, thus ensuring smooth and balanced ch'i flow. If not, residents may be startled, affecting their ch'i, making them nervous and jumpy. This in turn affects their personal relationships and performance at work. The unbalancing of occupants' ch'i will create both health and personality problems.

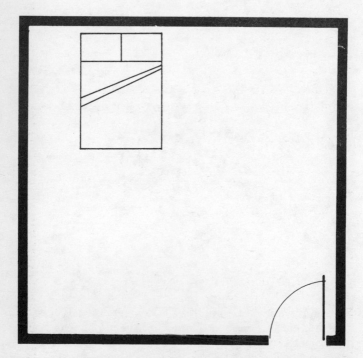

GOOD BED PLACEMENT

A bed should be catercorner to the door for the widest perspective and the ability to see anyone who enters.

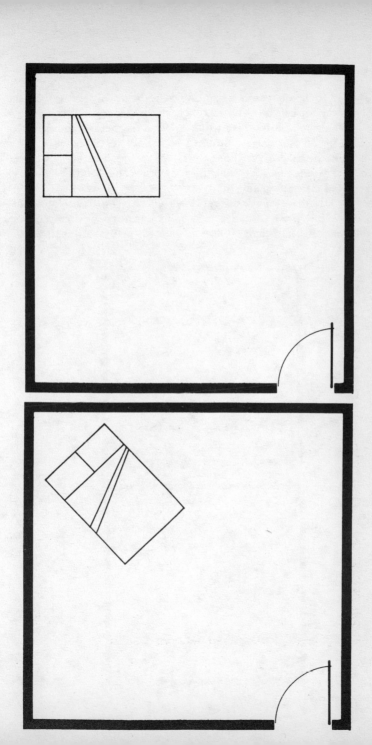

1. If, for some reason, a bed cannot lie diagonally across from the door, a mirror can be hung to reflect the entrance.

2. This bed position is further endangered because it resembles a coffin in the mortuary, waiting to be buried. In China, as in other countries, the corpse is traditionally taken out feet first. Hang a crystal ball or a windchime between the foot of the bed and the door to alleviate the negative effects.

3.–4. In these bedrooms, residents will be overly conscious of the door, and any noise will alert them in an awkward, unbalanced way, ultimately affecting their lives and performance far away from the bedroom.

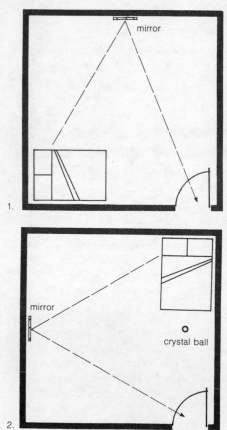

BED PLACEMENT CURES

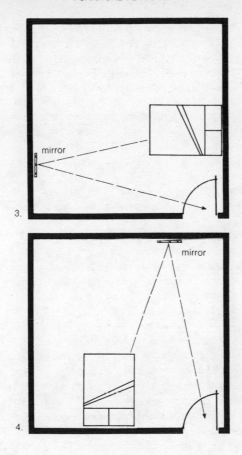

3.

4.

Kitchen

In the kitchen, feng shui experts pay most attention to the location of the stove and the rice cooker. A kitchen represents wealth: the Chinese word for food *(ts'ai)* sounds the same as the word for wealth. The logic follows a positive cycle: food feeds a person's health and effectiveness; therefore, the better the food, the more capable the person and the larger his potential income, which will, in turn, improve the quality of his food. There can also be a negative cycle: the poorer the person, the worse the food; thus he will earn even less money.

Ideally, the chef should be aware of anyone entering, or residents' health, wealth, and personal relations will suffer. If a cook is surprised, a nervous chain reaction is set off. For instance, if a husband's affectionate hug startles his wife while she is chopping carrots or cooking over a hot stove, she may get angry; this will affect their relationship that night and reverberate in the office the next day. In a restaurant, if the master chef is startled, it will affect everything from the quality of the food to the waiters' attitudes and the customers' satisfaction.

The cook should work in a spacious, brightly lit, and well-ventilated area. A stove cramped in a corner will inhibit the chef's movements and ch'i flow, lowering the quality of food and thus harming the health, wealth, careers, and relationships of family members.

Symbolically, the stove also figures prominently in a home's finances. It should be clean and work smoothly so that money *(ts'ai)* can easily enter the home. If burners are clogged, business will be plagued with obstructions. Family prosperity can be influenced by the amount of use of burners: the more burners, the more money earned; if some burners are not regularly used, the family will not prosper.

CURE. Mirrors or reflective aluminum on walls behind and, if necessary, to the side of the stove will allow for a more peaceful atmosphere and smoother cooking movements. The reflection of anyone entering will allow for a less jumpy, happier chef. Also, the symbolically increased number of burners widens earnings even for small stoves. If a stove faces a windowed wall, though good scenery bestows positive effects on the chef, it is best to have a reflective strip to mirror the doorway, or to hang a wind chime or crystal ball in line with the stove and the door.

Photograph 5B shows a kitchen with a mirror that reflects intruders, creates a sense of added space next to the cramped stove, and symbolically doubles the burners.

Here are some other illustrated variations:

1. The stove position is very good. The chef can easily see anyone entering.

2. An island stove is best, providing a less cramped arrangement.

3. The stove position is bad for family stability and finances.

CURE. Hang a wind chime or crystal ball between the stove and the door.

4. This stove position is unlucky.

CURE. Install a mirror above the stove to reflect intruders.

5. The stove is both poorly placed and cramped, which can hurt occupants' careers.

CURE. Hang mirrors on walls as shown.

6. This arrangement is bad.

CURE. Place a mirror on the side wall. The mirror also symbolically increases the number of burners.

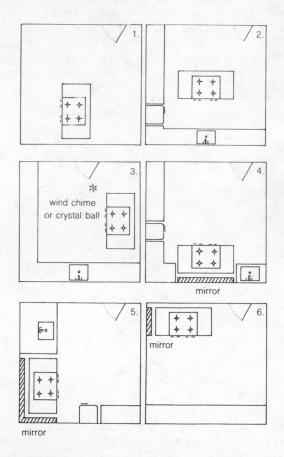

KITCHENS

Dining Room

Feng shui experts evaluate the dining area's position in the same way as the kitchen; it should not be too close to the entrance, or guests will eat and run. If this is the case, screen it from the initial view of those entering with doors or beaded curtains; even a crystal ball serves as a symbolic screen. An honored guest should sit facing the door.

Dining rooms.

1. This one is good if it is large. If the room is cramped and there are no other doors or windows, add mirrors to the walls. Mirrors also symbolically double dishes and wealth (see photograph 12).

2. This room is fine with the folding doors, if it is a restaurant. If the room is in a home, however, keep the folding doors open or they will close off professional development.

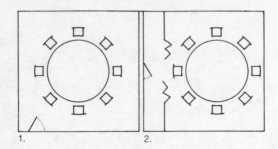

DINING ROOMS

Table shapes.

1.–3. Good shapes.

4. A rectangle is good if it is not too long.

5.–6. A dining table that is missing corners is unlucky.

7. One exception to the "no-corners" rule is a true octagon table—a very auspicious shape.

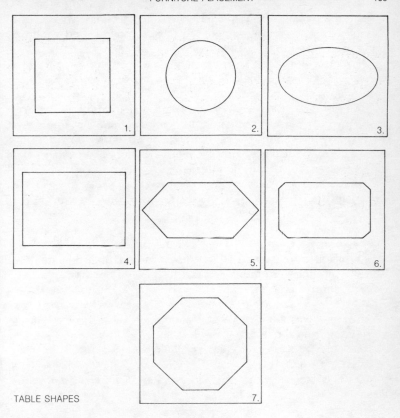

TABLE SHAPES

Living Room

In general, both the hosts and guests should face the door—but not in a direct line with it. The guests should sit in the "commanding" (c) position, catercorner to the door, and the host to the side, in a "safe" (s) position for a wide view of room and door (see illustrations pp. 110–111).

Furniture arrangement is important. Comfort and hospitality depend on good common sense. For example, geometric arrangements give a formal impression, while clustering creates cozy warmth. One matron on New York's Upper East Side found her parties less confrontational when she moved a bench facing the sofa to form an L with it.

In photograph 8A, auspiciously arranged sectional sofas create part of a ba-gua. In photograph 8B, mirrors on recessed windows bring in increased light and city views.

Fireplaces are warm and auspicious, but furniture too close to a fireplace, or facing it, should be offset by a mirror above or plants on each side of it. In photograph 9, the furniture grouping is conversational, faces the entrance, and is at a safe distance from the fireplace. A mirror provides a reflection of the entrance and the fireplace is auspiciously flanked by plants. Photograph 10 shows how floor-to-ceiling mirrors enhance a living room in a number of ways: they draw in river views; they visually double the space; they bring in more light; they hide a bedroom suite behind a mirrored door panel; they resolve an L-shaped apartment where the master bedroom juts outside the entrance door.

Some living room variations.

1–6. These are the best arrangements. With living room number 3, make sure the furniture is not too close to the fireplace. It is best to hang a mirror above the fireplace and install plants on either side.

7. The couch is too close to the door and faces away from it. (The couches in rooms number 3 and 4 should also be moved a foot or more away from the door.)

8. This arrangement is not good because the furniture is all oriented toward the fireplace.

9. This ba-gua arrangement is both auspicious and conversational.

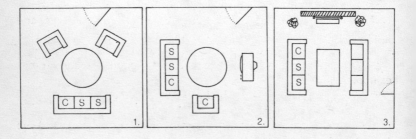

LIVING ROOMS

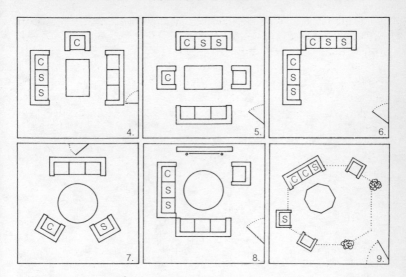

Bathroom

The bathroom, a place where water—symbolic of money—enters and leaves, represents occupants' internal plumbing and finances. Avoid placing the toilet opposite the door so that you see it when you enter, or residents may suffer financial losses, health disorders, or miscarriages. A hidden toilet is best (see photograph 7A).

CURE. Either place the toilet at the farthest point from the door, or construct a cubicle or curtain that shields the toilet from anyone entering. Other remedies are to hang a wind chime between the door and the toilet or to install a mirror on the outside of the door.

A bathroom should be bright and open, not cramped. Pale bathroom walls, such as blue, green, or peach, help maintain marital and family harmony. Photograph 7B shows a bathroom with a toilet inconspicuously placed behind the door, and mirrored walls which enlarge the space and bring in beneficent park views. Here are some other examples.

1.–2. These are the best bathroom arrangements.

3. This is the worst bathroom situation.

CURE. Install a barrier—a beaded curtain or a screen—to shield the toilet from the door.

4. This is bad, but can be cured in similar ways to number 3, above.

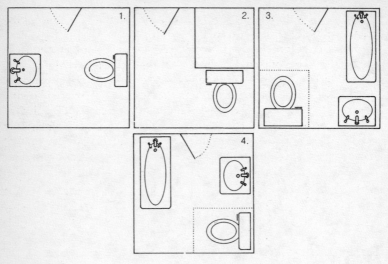

BATHROOMS

Lighting

While lamps and lights are often used as basic cures in feng shui to correct imbalances and activate and recirculate ch'i, the general lighting of a place can affect the moods, attitudes, and effectiveness of residents. Lights and lamps symbolize the sun and are considered essential for healthy, smooth circulation of ch'i—the brighter the better. (If a bulb burns out, replace it with one that is as bright or brighter.) There are exceptions to this. Although a dark home can be depressing to residents, sometimes low lights can help a restaurant's business. For instance, a feng shui expert who visited Elaine's, a celebrity hangout in New York, commented that the dark atmosphere made the mood "mellow" and relaxing. On the other hand, he said, at Auntie Yuan, another New York restaurant, spotlights aimed at small flower vases act as miniature suns "bringing up both the chi of diners and the luck of the restaurant." (See photograph 16C.)

Wall and Furniture Color

Wall and furniture color depend on a home or an office's size and lighting. As a rule, if the house or business is large or enjoys a lot of light, the colors of walls and furniture can be either dark or light.

However, if lighting is not very strong or the home is small, light colors will enliven the space.

Specific colors can enhance certain home and office situations. In the home, bedrooms and bathrooms should be pastel colors: blue, pink, or green. A jeweler should avoid yellow decor. This is because of an old Chinese saying, "An aging man is similar to a yellowing pearl," which implies that at a certain point both lose their value. A seaside cottage, fish store, or seafood restaurant does well with green decor—the color of live lobsters, shrimp, and crabs, the fruit of money-bearing water. Red decor, the color of cooked—and therefore dead—seafood, is not advisable in this case. Red, in general, is an auspicious color.

BUSINESS AND WORK PLACES

Office

To many Chinese, feng shui is essential in the art of business management. Indeed, now that Western corporations are incorporating power strategies from the East (samurai business practices and boardroom kung-fu), feng shui offers another financial edge over competitors. Western and Oriental banks, restaurants, and corporations throughout Asia and in the United States consult feng shui experts. One executive vice-president at Citibank comments, "We always have someone call in a feng shui man to check out our Asian offices—if we didn't our Chinese staff would probably quit." Indeed, one Citibank client joked that earnings might improve if they forsook feng shui, thus cutting massive expenses out of their budget. But Citibank is not alone; Chase Asia, Paine Webber, McKinsey and Company, the Morgan Bank, and the offices of the *Asian Wall Street Journal* all use feng shui.

A few months after Chase Asia's manager—who ignored a feng shui man's warnings—was killed in a plane crash in Kuala Lumpur, Chase relocated. Bank officials cite the local staff's insistence on feng shui as one reason for the move. The manager's unlucky office aside, Chase's old building itself was a feng shui nightmare. Besides the ominous, coffin-shaped windows, the high-rise overlooked a graveyard in Happy Valley. Today, the *Asian Wall Street Journal* occupies the building, and superstitious but savvy staff insisted on feng shui protective measures.

The Hong Kong and Shanghai Bank paid a feng shui expert five hundred dollars to advise on the design of its chairman's temporary office while construction of their new (feng shui–approved) headquarters was under way. They even relied on feng shui advice to decide when and where to temporarily relocate the bronze lions that flanked the old building entrance, and what direction they should face. When opening a bank branch, they employ a feng shui man to choose a proper date, approve the site and direction of the entrance, and officiate at the opening ceremonies.

"We recently used one in situating our new headquarters in Hong Kong," comments Donald Dougherty, the bank's vice-president of corporate relations. "And that is why we are considered to have the finest feng shui in Hong Kong; thus the Chinese hold us in such high regard." Norman Foster, the architect of what can claim the honor of being the world's most expensive building, consulted a feng shui expert during all design phases.

Indeed, when the headquarters opened in early 1986, the feng shui priest was on hand to help officiate at the more sacred aspects of the ceremony. (Even so, the Chinese claim it has bad feng shui. Some have even removed their accounts, fearing that because there are more descending than ascending escalators, their money will run down and out the door and their savings will be lost.)

When McKinsey and Company, a New York-based management consulting group opened their Hong Kong office in 1986, they chose the building, floor, and office by lucky numbers—most had auspicious eights in them. During the planning stages, the architect suggested they hire a feng shui expert, who chose where the reception area should be and in what direction desks should face. He also suggested using red in the lobby, and placing a rock in the corner of the manager's office. According to the manager, no Chinese would work there without a feng shui expert's approval. "We did it as a cultural necessity," he commented. "I can't say it aided our financial successes," he added, "but, our staff likes it, and our clients tend to come to the office, because they feel it has good omens and atmosphere. Our own image is heightened by showing we understand their cultural needs."

Not only the Chinese ascribe to feng shui's wisdom. Several American businessmen and bankers returning from Far Eastern assignments have adopted feng shui, convinced that without it they won't succeed.

William S. Doyle, executive vice-president of a New York advertising agency, who sent blueprints of his sixteen-thousand-square-foot office to a feng shui expert in Hong Kong, explains, "People don't understand, it's three thousand years of common sense. There's also an art, a form, and a reason to the way it's done. It's practical and pragmatic—not just happenstance, with some crazy decorator coming in and shoving around furniture."

Desk Position

In any business, the first feng shui consideration is the manager's office. The Chinese believe an entire company's fortunes rest on the good siting of its president and manager. The manager should sit in the most commanding position to assert authority over his employees. Authority generally emanates from the corner office farthest from the entrance. The rules are basically *Power!* Chinese-style, predating and coinciding with power-placement concepts in a recent book on corporate hierarchies and power plays.* Indeed, one executive who was constantly at odds with his partner in a small Los Angeles marketing firm found that when the company moved and he had the corner office, things started going his way. One partner in the New York architect's office of Skidmore, Owings & Merrill refused to move into a new office, on the advice of a feng shui expert. It was an inaccessible room where anyone wishing to enter it would first have to walk through a narrow hallway that zigzagged. "He told me the occupant of the office would always fight his colleagues." Now auspiciously ensconced in an office with easier access, she says her co-workers marvel at her office power. Just as the most important furniture in a home should be placed catercorner to the door, so should a desk in an office. It is the power position for maximum control, concentration, and authority. Workers sitting there will have the greatest scope of vision and feel in command of their situation. It is the best place for expanding business. The position also avoids the likelihood of being startled at one's work—an experience that unbalances ch'i and impairs work by making one jumpy, easy to upset, and partially distracted. If a desk cannot be catercorner to the door, install a mirror to reflect anyone who enters . Mirrors can also draw in money-endowing river views and visually increase the area of small offices (see photograph 14).

---

* Michael Korda. *Power: How to Get It, How to Use It* (New York: Ballantine, 1976).

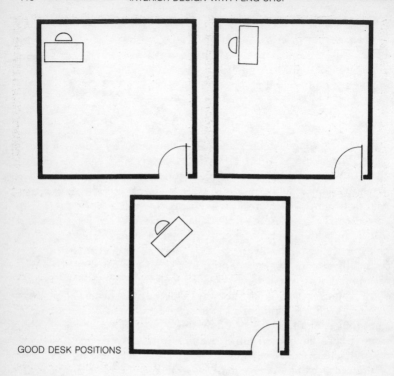

GOOD DESK POSITIONS

There are countless stories of the effectiveness of correct desk placement. One instance is an employee of an art magazine who worked there for two years without getting a raise. She also had no boyfriend. In frustration, she sought feng shui advice. The expert advised her to move her desk away from the wall, so that she had a commanding view of the door. Within a day or two, she said, she felt a positive change, and within a month she not only received a raise, but also had a host of suitors. (When she had to move her office, and was prevented from shifting her desk to see the door, she lost her job and her newfound popularity.)

A New York book editor who suffered from overwork and shingles had an expert assess his office. His desk faced away from the door. A week after he moved his desk to face the door, both work and shingles cleared up. "I don't know whether it's coincidence, but it's remarkable how much better I feel," he commented. Five months later, when he was appointed editor-in-chief of adult books, he re-

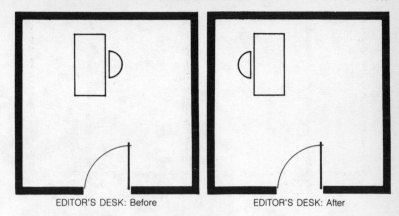

EDITOR'S DESK: Before   EDITOR'S DESK: After

marked, "I suppose I can credit feng shui. It's been so successful for me that other editors are moving their desks around too."

Turning one's back on any door—even a fire door or a backdoor— can bring bad luck. Many things will happen behind one's back. An employee of a California bank moved her seat away from the back door on the advice of a feng shui expert. Shortly afterwards, the next person in line lost her job (see illustration below).

Sitting with one's back to the door is asking for trouble. In the manager's office of a large California corporation, three consecutive supervisors not only failed, but also were demoted within six months of their appointments. (See top illustration p. 118.)

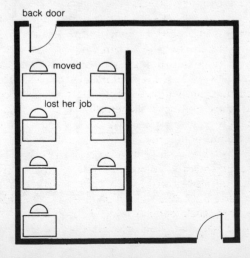

BANK OFFICE

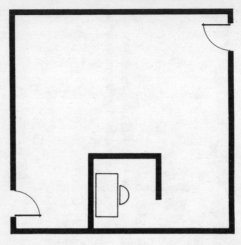

ILL-APPOINTED MANAGER'S OFFICE

Avoid having interior glass windows behind you. One entrepreneur, a trained engineer and contractor, bought a wholesale bakery on the Monterey Peninsula that was nearly bankrupt; three owners in five years had consecutively been forced to sell out. He faced labor

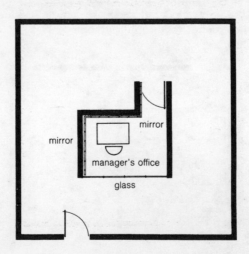

BAKERY FACTORY

problems: disgruntled workers with low morale and productivity, sloppy workmanship, and low-quality merchandise. Using both ru-shr —his own business ideas—and chu-shr cures, he turned the company around. Among the feng shui changes were mirrors that he installed to double business, smooth the flow of ch'i, and resolve the uncertainty of a window behind his desk. (He also adjusted the "helpful people" area (see chapter 8). Shortly afterward, one of his bakers concocted a new high-quality product that they produced in bulk and that sold well; a maverick in the business offered his services, business doubled, and morale increased. The owner comments, "I'm not sure why, but feng shui works."

Self-image and the attitudes of others are affected by desk positions. If the boss sits too close to the door, he will be treated or thought of as an underling and lose respect, while the secretary will be insubordinate and run the office from a position of power.

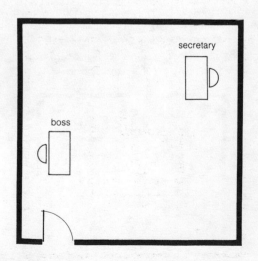

The secretary runs this office.

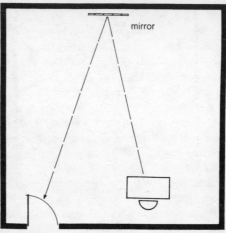

OFFICE OF EARLY LEAVER

Workers sitting close to the door will leave work before the end of the workday and avoid working overtime. They will pay too much attention to the door, and constantly think of returning home.

CURE. Hang a mirror to take the worker's attention away from the door.

A stressful situation for any underling is one in which the boss sits directly in front of his employee, either facing him or with his back to him, unsettling the employee's ch'i.

CURE. Place a bowl of water, with or without fish, or a crystal ball on the desk to create a more peaceful atmosphere.

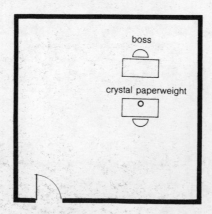

AWKWARD BOSS/UNDERLING PLACEMENT

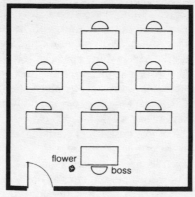

CLASSROOM-STYLE OFFICE

Some offices look a bit like classrooms. This is a situation in which the boss sits near the door, like a proctor who makes sure students don't sneak out. While the boss may enjoy a broad view, this position makes his or her ch'i jumpy and irascible. The resulting bad temper is detrimental for the entire office, and work and morale will be low. CURE. Install a bright flower—fresh or artificial—between the boss and the door to attract his or her attention, making the boss aware of those entering and exiting, and as protection.

In smaller offices and shared studies, desk arrangement can create auspicious conditions. After the president of Vintage North West, a company promoting Washington State wines, moved desks to create a ba-gua symbol, business improved substantially. "It was dramatic," comments Lila Gault, the firm's vice-president. "Within a month ev-

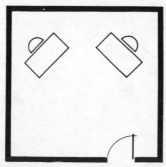

BA-GUA DESK ARRANGEMENT

erything came together. While we weren't struggling before, there seemed to be an infusion of positive energy. It had a positive impact on business within the office. We communicated much better."

At the suggestion of a feng shui expert, a New York artist moved her desk from her bedroom to the third and top floor of her house —the head or commanding position. She placed her desk catercorner to the door on the diagonal (see photograph 15) and since then her career has taken off and her work has received unforeseen recognition. "Whenever I sit at this desk I feel confident and always send my show invitations out from here," she said.

If a hallway (often seen as a dragon's mouth) or any strong force such as a corner or powerful person aims at the desk, sending strong ch'i your way, hang a wind chime over the edge of the desk or place a crystal ball on the desktop in the line of the hallway. A vice-president at Morgan Bank whose desk was exposed to the managing director whenever he left his office said he felt more confident after he placed a crystal paperweight on his desk angled to protect himself. Plants can also provide protection.

With an understanding of balance and some knowledge of feng shui rules, businesspeople can feng shui their own offices. A liquor wholesaler, a magazine editor, and the head of an ailing philanthropic organization all reported vast improvements in their individual performance and the fortunes of their companies after turning their desks to face the door. The last of these said that, within a day of moving his desk, he received a $20,000 grant that he had applied for long before and had given up on. The next day he received an unsolicited grant. "I'm nailing my desk down," he said with a smile.

Some offices are open-plan designs, with immovable desks. If you face a wall, hang a mirror on the wall or rest one on the desk. If a mirror is frowned on in the office, surreptitiously slip one into the desk drawer facing the desired direction as a symbolic protection.

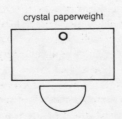

crystal paperweight

EXPOSED DESK

Computers

According to modern feng shui experts, computers affect ch'i. Computers can be good, enlivening, and stimulating to the office. They can raise wisdom and knowledge. The computer worker, however, should face the door or he or she will suffer from stress and neurosis after a while. A New York bank executive found his work less stressful and new business easier to attain once he moved his computer, at a feng shui expert's suggestion, from a position that placed his back to the door to one facing the door. "I feel less nervous, more in control, and that I can hold on to business prospects which before seemed to elude me," he explained.

Cash Registers

In stores and restaurants, the cash register should be positioned to give the cashier a good view of the door, to be both receptive to clients and on guard against thieves. A mirror hung behind the register will help to increase profits by drawing in business and symbolically doubling the contents of the cash register. In a restaurant, mirrors hung behind bars and wine racks double the amount of liquor sold and create a sense of depth. Other attractive additions, such as plants, lighting, aquariums, flowers, and colors also serve a symbolic function and attract customers (see photograph 16B).

POLITICS

Although making money seems to be the primary earthly goal of feng shui, the Chinese have long used it for political power as well. Most likely, the first office ever arranged by a feng shui adept was that of an ancient Chinese emperor. For thousands of years, such specialists divined where an emperor should sit and face to exert the most control, power, and righteousness over the realm. The Chinese believed that the emperor's seat represented the country's strength, and that if the emperor fared well, the nation would follow suit. (In Washington, several high-ranking politicians have consulted Lin Yun, presumably for feng shui purposes.)

After studying a picture of the Oval Office in the White House, one feng shui expert suggested a couple of modifications that might improve the fortunes of both the President and the United States.

For instance, he said, the President sits too close to the wall behind him. To resolve this imbalance, the desk should be moved forward four to five inches. "This will not only improve his reputation and power—help his ch'i rise and circulate—but also widen his perspective, opening his mind to new ways to solve the nation's problems. This will obviously affect the country's future for the better." He added that it would be good not only for the President's personal health and safety, but for his peace and clarity of mind.

He also suggested moving the President's plush white sofas on a slant to create part of a ba-gua shape. The style of the seats are also important. Solid-backed chairs are best for ensuring that advisers and friends will be more supportive.

And as a crowning touch, he suggested hanging an ornament above the center window. "A red flower, picture, or light will do, but the presidential insignia would be best." No matter who the President is, his seat represents the country's strength. The ornament will raise the President's ch'i and that of the country. If he doesn't install the insignia, the President will rule, but not necessarily control, the country.

MYSTICAL BURGLAR ALARM

Feng shui is also used for security. After a California bank was robbed a decade ago, its owner sought feng shui help. The expert recommended installing a bell on the door to the teller's work area to ring each time it was opened. As a primitive but effective alarm, the bell, he said, would unnerve would-be robbers. Milton Glaser, the graphic designer, after being robbed six times, installed a red clock and a tank with six black fish as a sort of mystical security system. Both he and the bank have been robber-free ever since.

Another mystical means to safeguard a business is to place near the cash register a vase—symbolizing peace—with a red ribbon wrapped around it, and to hang a bamboo flute tied with a red ribbon above it. The flute acts both as a symbolic sword protecting profits and patrons and as a funnel conducting ch'i upward through the sections of the flute to help improve business (see photograph 16A). (If the flutes are hung the wrong way, conducting ch'i downward, business will falter. This happened to a store in California; business picked up when the flutes were turned right side up.) If the outside area is dangerous, a series of two doors can help filter out destructive exterior ch'i.

8

BA-GUA

BA-GUA

In addition to applying practical methods to enhance one's environment, one can improve ch'i by applying a philosophical principle—the *I Ching* ba-gua—to a plot of land, a house, a room, a piece of furniture, or a person. Though rooted in ancient mysticism, it can be applied to everyday life in a more or less practical way. The whole process is

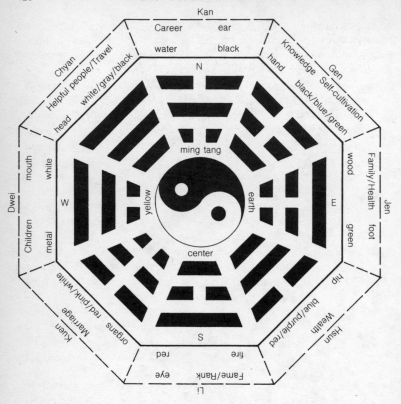

THE BA-GUA AND ITS CORRESPONDING ELEMENTS, BODY PARTS, COLORS, AND LIFE
SITUATIONS.

based on an internalized ba-gua shape. It is an octagon divided into
eight life situations—marriage, fame, wealth, family, knowledge, career, helpful people, and children. Black Hat sect experts simply
memorize the ba-gua and superimpose it on rooms, buildings, and
even beds. They use the ba-gua both as a guide to interpret a person's
life and problems and as a cure to resolve them. Since everyone bumps
into trouble and misfortune—in marriage, work, or with children—

the ba-gua becomes a map of one's life condition. The Chinese believe that an understanding of the ba-gua and its relationship to houses, bodies, and luck enables them to mystically manipulate their destiny.

Many stories are told about tipping fate's hand by "adjusting" the ba-gua. A California student claims she was accepted at the college of her choice after activating the "knowledge" area in her bedroom. An entrepreneur said business improved substantially when he made adjustments in the "helpful people" position in his office. A restaurateur altered already complete renovations when a feng shui expert advised her to put the cash register in the "wealth" spot. This all may be self-fulfilling prophecy, but many swear by it.

The application of the ba-gua is simple: If a person's marriage is having problems, he might adjust the "marriage" position in his bedroom. Or if a businessman wants to improve his finances, he might enhance the "wealth" area of his office or home.

Any of the Nine Basic Cures—mirrors, wind chimes, light, and so on (see chapter 3)—can be used to adjust or enhance an area of one's room or life. When adjusting the ba-gua positions, these nine methods are generally interchangeable, depending on individual needs and tastes. For example, if a person wants more money, he might install a plant or fishtank in the money or *hsun* position of his office, or maybe a wind chime in the *hsun* area of his bedroom. To rise in the corporate ladder, he might install a heavy machine or computer in the career or *kan* spot.

One elderly San Francisco resident hopes she has left nothing to fate by reinforcing each of the eight areas or *gua* in her bedroom. In the marriage area she installed a crystal ball and a string of eighty-one smaller crystals. They hang directly in front of a western window, filling the room at sunset with many rainbows, thus encouraging an already long marriage. She has wind chimes in the "children" and "family" positions to safeguard offspring—who refuse to use feng shui themselves—and to intervene in petty family bickering. In the "helpful people" area, she hangs a knickknack shelf where she leaves petitions to the gods and the Buddha that all her wishes be answered. In the "fame" position is a silk flower, in the "wealth" spot hang two flutes, and in the "career" area are pictures of her grandchildren. In the "knowledge" area—the bedroom's entrance, which happens to be slanted—she hangs nine firecrackers above the door, thus ensuring for her husband, a retired professor, continued scholarship and for the family deepened knowledge and awareness.

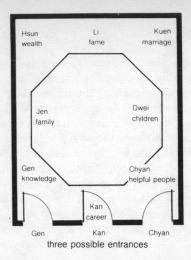

Gen   Kan   Chyan

THREE-DOOR BA-GUA   three possible entrances

For ba-gua calculations, in Black Hat sect practice, the door is pivotal.* The door, literally translated, is the "mouth of ch'i"—*ch'i kou.* Its position determines where the eight gua are situated in a room. No matter how seldom an entrance is used, it is still considered the main door to calculate ba-gua positions and house shape requirements. If the side door is used more often, even though it will influence your entrance and exit, it will not become the basis of ba-gua orientation.

When the ba-gua is superimposed on a room or a house, the entrance will fall into one of three possible positions—three gua of the octagon. This depends on whether it is in the center or to the side of a wall. If the door is in the center, it is *kan*, career; if it opens to the right of center, it is Chyan, helpful people, meaning both underlings and patrons; if it opens to the left of center, the door is in the *gen*, or knowledge position. This method is called "three-door ba-gua."

*Black Hat sect feng shui's use of the *I Ching* deviates from traditional practices where a fixed ba-gua is superimposed on homes, plots, and rooms in order to raise their ch'i. Traditionally, Li, for example, is always south. As a result, many businesspeople in Hong Kong seek to buy homes with doors in the southeast corner, the traditional "wealth spot." Unlike traditional feng shui, cardinal directions make no difference in Black Hat sect feng shui. Traditional feng shui experts practice a sort of astrology of the earth. To calculate what direction the entrance, bed, or desk should face they tally their client's birthdate with cosmic elements embossed on an ancient and complicated geomancer's compass. They also use this "cosmic compass" to divine ch'i lines or geographic features, to site a home, grave, or bed, as well as to discern the auspiciousness and compatability of a place or a person. For example, a New York advertising executive hoping to merge his firm with a larger one was told it wouldn't happen until his door faced west. After he and his family coincidentally moved to a home with this recommended setup, a merger occurred.

The ba-gua can be used to adjust ill-shaped plots of land, homes, and rooms. It can be superimposed on any lot, house, or room, no matter what the shape. By using the ba-gua, the feng shui expert can easily discern areas of trouble in occupants' lives.

Rooms and apartments present an endless variety of shapes. The Chinese elongate and shorten the ba-gua in order to apply it to each space. An irregularly shaped house or one missing a corner may indicate a shortcoming in the corresponding area of the occupant's life. Number 3, for instance, is missing its career part, so occupants may have job problems.

While the ba-gua can be applied to shapes to resolve imbalances in the shape or to enhance certain areas of the occupants' lives, some people have gone so far as to create octagonal rooms. Thus all eight gua are emphasized and balanced and the octagon itself is the most auspicious shape of all. Mr. K's, a well-known restaurant in Wash-

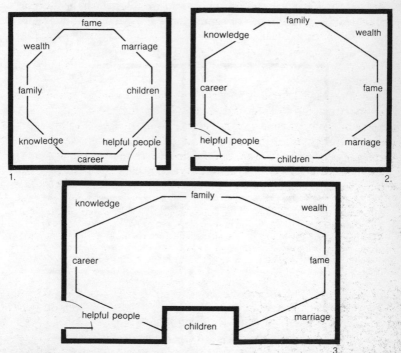

The ba-gua applies to rooms of any shape or size.

ington, is based on a recurring ba-gua theme: the outer banquettes and the inner ones both create octagons. In addition, on the advice of a feng shui expert, the owners placed the stove and the cash register in the "wealth" and "helpful people" areas. "We asked him where the best ch'i spots of the ba-gua were situated," explains Lola Kao, wife of the owner, Johnny Kao.

L-SHAPES AND U-SHAPES

L-shaped homes, offices, or rooms can present occupants with a multitude of problems. They connote something incomplete or un-balanced—as though part of the ba-gua were missing. Depending on the size of the "missing" gua, one, two, or three areas can be lacking in residents' lives. Here are a number of examples:

These shapes are each missing at least one gua. House 1 lacks knowledge. House 2 is missing the marriage area. In house 3, both the marriage and the children will have troubles. In house 4, marriage, children, and fame—or reputation—will all have shortcomings.

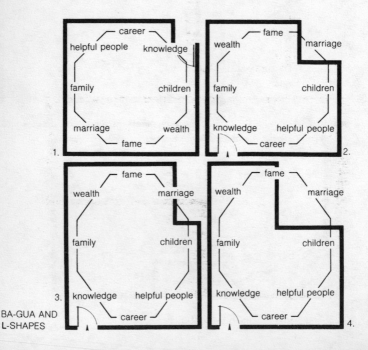

BA-GUA AND
L-SHAPES

House shapes number 5 and 6 present additional complications. In houses where wings jut out from the front door line, residents will find areas in their lives lacking—helpful people in house 5, and knowledge, career, and family in house 6. Occupants also may find, if the kitchen or the bedroom is located in the wing, that they will sleep or eat out all the time, creating more strains on family relationships. In addition, the wing will block out ch'i and opportunities. Thus, residents' own ch'i will become unbalanced and their business success will be limited.

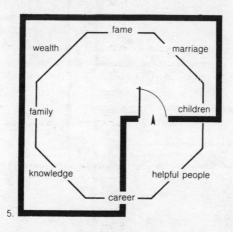

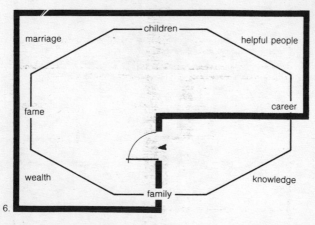

BA-GUA AND L-SHAPED WINGS BEHIND ENTRANCE

Some L-shaped buildings and rooms can bring luck to residents. This auspiciousness depends on the size of the ell and the position of the door. If the wing is less than half the width or length of the house, it is considered a positive addition. House 7 is particularly good for scholarship. Shape 8 will enjoy much wealth, and 9 will house a good marriage.

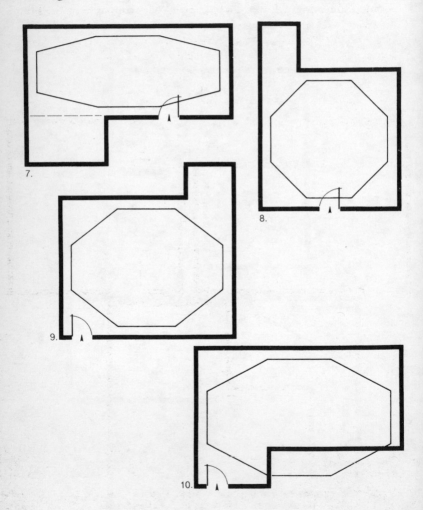

BA-GUA AND SMALL L-SHAPED WINGS

When the entrance of a home, office, or room is in the small wing, the shape will lack two guas. In house 10, for example, the residents will have problems in their careers and people will be less than helpful.

In general, to balance the ba-gua of L-shaped houses, use any of the Nine Basic Cures:

1. To resolve this shape, add a mirror to either or both sides of the missing corner to extend the space symbolically.

2.–3. To adjust the missing wealth area in these houses, either add a wind chime to either side or hang a crystal ball at the corner's edge.

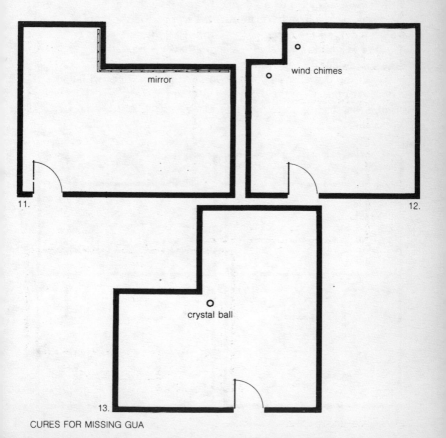

CURES FOR MISSING GUA

Ba-gua adjustments in a businessperson's home can be as effective as those in the office. An accountant in Miami, whose L-shaped home lacked the wealth area, found business increased substantially after she squared off the shape by installing a small spotlight in the wealth area and aimed the light at the roof.

As with L-shaped houses, wings of U-shaped buildings can have positive or negative effects, depending on their size and door placement. The wings can create a void in their center, and thus a loss for occupants. If they are small enough, however, wings can be seen as assets. Residents of house 1 will enjoy good scholarship and help from others. Bear in mind that it may be troublesome for family relations if the master bedroom or kitchen is located in a wing. Shapes 2, 3, and 4, however, are all missing a gua. Shape 2's residents will find that their scholarship, family relations, and to some extent their finances will founder. (If the entrance were in the U, the two wings would be considered additions.) People living in shapes 3 and 4 will have a hard time succeeding in their careers.

CURE. If the U-shape is a house, connect the two wings with a line of red paint or bushes. If the shape is an apartment, ritually seal the inside of all doors leading to the outside as well as the bedroom door (see Appendix 1).

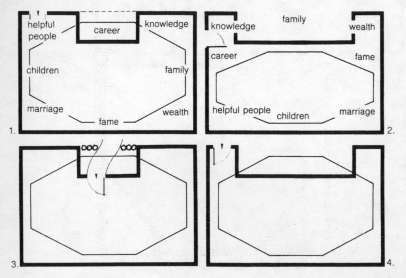

BA-GUA AND U-SHAPES

SLANTS

A slant—as mentioned in chapter 6—is unfortunate in any home since it portends an unpleasant, unforeseen happening or catastrophe.

Some slants made by a fifth wall affect rooms by creating an extra angle and thus an irregular and unbalanced shape. Slants are often structural necessities to make room for existing stairs or air-conditioning systems, and the resultant missing corner of the ba-gua should be compensated. In the first illustration, a slanted fifth wall cuts out part of the knowledge area.

CURES. Add three complementary slanted walls to the room to create an auspicious octagon, or hang a large mirror or a bamboo flute on the slanted wall to allow ch'i to penetrate it. (See below.)

Structures with an entire slanted wall are problematic and incomplete. A slanted wall will affect two guas. House 1, for example, is bad for children and opportunities for outside help. Room 2 can harm your reputation and create disharmony in your marriage. In room 3, fame and finances will suffer. (See illustration p. 136.)

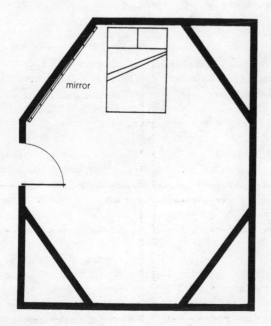

BA GUA AND SLANTED FIFTH WALL

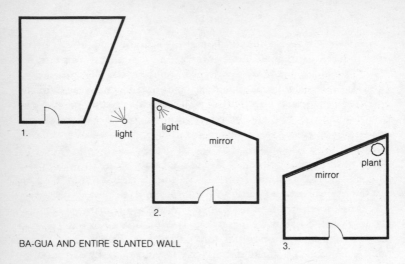

1.

light

light

mirror

2.

mirror

plant

3.

BA-GUA AND ENTIRE SLANTED WALL

CURES.

1. A house with a slant can be resolved in the garden: install a lamp to square off the exterior shape.

2.–3. For apartments, hang a mirror on the slanted wall (see photograph 13), the bigger the mirror the better, or install a light or plant in the acute-angled corner to encourage ch'i to circulate.

Corners, closets, columns, and bathrooms can also unbalance a room by cutting a piece out of it and affecting a part of the ba-gua. In one San Francisco home where the bathroom had a corner in the marriage position, the wife hung pictures of red and gold fish to adjust the gua, so that her marriage would go "swimmingly."

The position of a bathroom in a home can affect the corresponding area of a person's life or body. For example, if the bathroom is in the wealth position of the house, money will be flushed away.

CURE. Hang mirrors on a side of the corner to obscure the jutting edge and resolve the gua, hang a crystal ball or wind chime on either side, or grow a vine up the corner. Another cure is to mix ju-sha with ninety-nine drops newly opened wine. Then pour the mixture down the toilet (see Appendix 1). Other examples: If the kitchen is in the wealth area, food (symbolizing earnings) will be abundant; a study in the knowledge area is ideal for scholarship; a bed in the marriage position of the bedroom will bring domestic harmony. In the children's room, put beds in the "children" area to make sure they behave.

BUSINESSES AND THE BA-GUA

The Chinese believe you can encourage and develop business by adjusting the office interior ba-gua. Here the pertinent areas to develop include career, wealth, fame, and helpful people, in that order. In a company, the ba-gua of the president's office is more important than the ba-gua of the company as a whole.

In a store or a restaurant, a cash register optimally should be catercorner to the door, so that the cashier can see customers come and go, ensuring smooth profits. Ideally, the register should sit in the wealth position, with a mirror behind it to draw ch'i, opportunity, and money toward it. If the cash register cannot sit in the wealth position, use one of the Nine Basic Cures, i.e., a mirror, a lamp, or a machine such as a jukebox or television, in the wealth position to compensate for the register's absence.

The career and helpful-people positions are also good areas to store money. The position chosen for a cash register will determine the nature of profits. Income from a register in the wealth position of a restaurant, for example, will come from the food. If, on the other hand, the register is sited in the helpful-people position, profits will derive from its popularity, increased customers, and unexpected help. A register in the knowledge position will bring profits from hard work and business savvy, such as special promotions.

For example, at Auntie Yuan, a successful restaurant in New York (see photograph 16C), the cash register is situated in the "helpful people" position, out of view from the entrance and so more protected from robbers. A strategically placed bamboo flute creates an auspicious ba-gua shape over the cash register and guards the restaurant. Mirrors behind the bar create the illusion of twice as many bottles and will symbolically double the amount of liquor sold.

To determine the ba-gua positions in a store or restaurant, use only the main functioning area, discounting unused wings or storage areas.

Slants that will drag down or obscure profits should be avoided. In one restaurant, the cash register was under a structural slant; the owners built a complementary slant to create a partial ba-gua shape.

Occupants of a Long Island, New York, home hung flutes angled to mimic both the auspicious ba-gua octagon and to augment the wealth and marriage areas of its propitiously arranged living room.

Floor-to-ceiling mirrors double the space and obscure the entrance to a family temple (see photograph 4).

The location of a room within a building can affect business. A feng shui expert strolling through a kitchen of Le Cirque, a restaurant in New York, commented that because the pastry section was in the wealth area, profits would be "sweet." Another restaurant's restrooms were in the wealth area, so the expert said that their profits would be "flushed away." Yet another restaurant's restrooms, located in the fame area, augured a reputation tainted with ill will and criticism.

CORNERS AND ANGLES

Sharp angles can threaten business, customers, and workers. As Flower Lounge, a restaurant in Milbrae, California, neared completion of its renovation, a feng shui expert suggested to its owners that they round out all sharp edges of their newly installed square columns, counters, and corners. Then they installed a sink in the wealth area. "I'd rather do it now than suffer later," commented Alice Wong, the young co-owner. "With the right environment, good food, price and service and feng shui advice, we'll do well." And indeed, since the restaurant opened in late 1984, it has thrived.

ENTRANCES

Business entrances and back doors should be wide and light. Generally, entrances should be in the career or helpful-people position; if not, these positions should be enhanced by one of the Nine Basic Cures. In late 1983, one Silicon Valley computer company suffering from slow business installed, on the advice of a feng shui expert, a fish tank under the stairs near the entrance of their rented building to help trapped ch'i circulate. They also installed two lights inside the door—at the helpful-people position—to raise opportunities. In only four weeks business was so good they bought the building.

Live fish, thriving in wealth-enhancing water, are also money-making devices in offices, businesses, and restaurants. For best results, stock your bowl or tank with nine fish—eight red and one black, or eight black and one red.

COLORS AND THE BA-GUA

Colors can be used to adjust the ch'i of a home or an office. A person can enhance aspects of his or her life by installing a complementary color in the corresponding ba-gua area. The five elements are used to figure out what color will benefit an area. By superimposing the five elements and their corresponding colors on the ba-gua, you can discern what colors can be applied to a room to enhance various areas (see the Five-Element Color Creative Cycle chart). When aligned with the ba-gua, family is wood or green, wealth is part green and part red, fame is fire or red, marriage is part red and part white, children is metal or white, helpful people is part white and part black, career is water or black, and knowledge is part black and part green. The center is earth or yellow. Thus, a person or business wanting to receive more recognition might—besides hiring a publicist—put something red in the fame position. Or if a family is at odds, one might set a green plant in the family position.

The Chinese increase their color options by applying the Five-Element Color Creative Cycle in another way as well. Red and green encourage wealth; green, red, and yellow develop fame; red and white enhance marriages; yellow, white, and black encourage children;

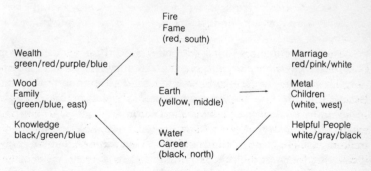

FIVE-ELEMENT COLOR CREATIVE CYCLE.

Fire
Fame
(red, south)

Wealth
green/red/purple/blue

Marriage
red/pink/white

Wood
Family
(green/blue, east)

Earth
(yellow, middle)

Metal
Children
(white, west)

Knowledge
black/green/blue

Water
Career
(black, north)

Helpful People
white/gray/black

This chart shows which colors can enhance a specific gua. For example, if you want to improve career opportunities, you can place something black (the career/water color), white (the metal color, which creates water/career), and green (the color of wood, which is fed by water) in the career area.

black and white bring helpful people; white, black, and green help
career; black and green deepen knowledge; black, green, and red help
the family. So the warring family can also install something black or
red in the family area, and the person seeking publicity can also use
green and yellow in the fame area.

When adjusting ch'i with colors, always reinforce the act with the
Three Secrets ritual (see Appendix 1).

FENG SHUI AND STAGES OF LIFE

Bedroom feng shui in particular can be adjusted according to
your stage of life. Because human ch'i is affected by the house, certain
modifications—chu-shr cures—can be made to the bedroom to balance and moderate ch'i—be it that of a child or of an old man.

Children should sleep in the *dwei*—children—position of their
bedroom. The nursery should be spacious and well lit, an open space
for lots of activity. A young child's ch'i is unstable, so he or she needs
room to move. Large pieces of furniture are malign obstacles in bedrooms, and can be particularly harmful to a child. They oppress and
unbalance the child's ch'i. A heavy piece near the door or next to the
child's bed may cause constant sprained ankles and broken bones.
CURE. To enhance the child's ch'i, put something white—a white
sheet, flowers, a stuffed animal, etc.—in the *dwei* spot. If the bed
cannot lie in the *dwei* position, install a lamp there.

Until he or she is thirteen or fourteen years old, a child's ch'i is
not only unstable and undeveloped, but also a bit misguided and
distracted.
CURE. Hang a moving object—mobile, wind chime, whirligig—or a
light at the child's eye level to raise and stimulate the ch'i in the mind.
Channeling ch'i upward will make the child smarter and more motivated. Colorful objects and fishbowls also enhance children's ch'i.
They should still sleep in the *dwei* position.

Fifteen- to twenty-two-year-olds need more peace and stability, so
items should be more fixed. Books in the bedroom or a library-studio
near the entrance would help to inspire their studies.
CURE. The bed or desk could be in the knowledge position; or place
something black, blue, or green or any of the Nine Basic Cures there.

While the child is in school, adjust the knowledge position. Once
he or she graduates, enhance the career or helpful-people position.

For married couples or those hoping to get married, place either
the bed or something red or white in the marriage position.

Older people should sleep in the family position. If they can't sleep there, place something green or one of the Nine Basic Cures in the money or fame position.

THE THREE HARMONIES

Another way to balance the ba-gua or to strengthen ba-gua positions is the Three Harmonies. The Three Harmonies uses four mystical triangles on an overlapping chart of the ba-gua, twelve astrological stems, and five elements.

The Three Harmonies can be used in any room. It particularly comes in handy when resolving or enhancing a house, room, or plot with additions.

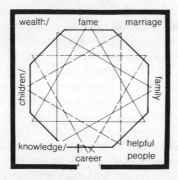

THE THREE HARMONIES

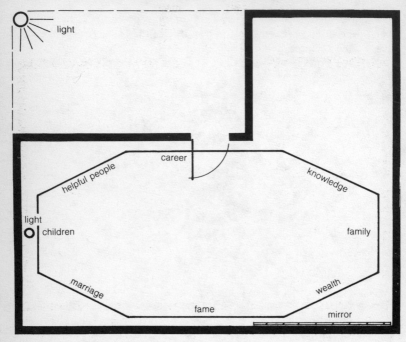

USING THE THREE HARMONIES

A home as illustrated, with a lopsided entrance area in the knowledge position may be long on scholarship but short on career and helpful people. This can be resolved a number of ways.

CURES.

1. Add a mirror to reflect the addition, creating a symbolic complementary addition and thus enhancing the wealth area.

2. Balance the shape with a lamppost, spotlight, or landscaping.

3. Use the Three Harmonies. Create a triangle by adjusting the wealth area and enhancing the children position.

4. Residents living here will enjoy good careers, but their knowledge may be lacking, and underlings will be less than helpful.

CURES.

1. Add mirrors to wall A.

2. Build complementary wings.

3. Use the Three Harmonies and add mirrors to areas b and c to create imaginary additions and thus develop the wealth and marriage areas.

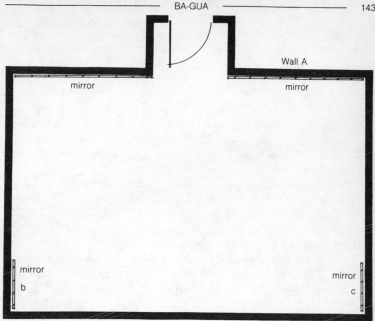

USING THE THREE HARMONIES

To balance or reinforce the ch'i of a gua, the two complementary angles of the mystical triangle can be adjusted. For example, if you want to help your children, use one of the Nine Basic Cures to tip the balance or enhance marriage and helpful-people areas. To improve family life, you could add a mirror either to the family position or to the two complementary angles, wealth and knowledge.

HOUSE-BODY RELATIONSHIPS

Feng shui experts often double as doctors. They feel that a home and its parts have a corresponding relationship to the human body. When imbalances in the home are remedied, the occupants' health will improve. What happens in the house may ultimately be reflected in residents' lives and bodies—and vice versa. Residents' health depends both on ch'i flowing smoothly and on a balancing of yin and yang.

A door is called *ch'i kou,* translated as "mouth of ch'i." In general, doors and windows are the body orifices. For example, if a door is blocked, residents may be constipated. If a windowpane is broken, residents' eyes, ears, and nose may have problems. The plumbing, gas, and electrical systems can be applied to occupants' circulation, breathing, and digestion. Gas leaks, clogged plumbing, and blown fuses can alter house ch'i and subsequently affect the welfare of occupants so that they will suffer. Thus, house maintenance is crucial.

As with the earth, thoughtless alterations made in a home or a business can threaten the occupants. It is similar to undergoing sloppy, unplanned surgery: the outcome may only be worse. So, care must be taken when making changes ranging from installing an air conditioner to renovating a bathroom.

Alterations must be done at the right time and place, and only after performing the Three Secrets ritual. (See Appendix 1.) There are countless stories directly relating broken arms and legs to cutting a tree branch, mowing the lawn, digging a ditch, or opening a skylight in the arm or leg position of a house on land plot.

Changes can also enhance a home, as in the case of a mirrored and lit skylight in a New York home, which is shaped like a Mongolian "hotpot" and heightens ch'i circulation. Placed at the "head" of the house and installed with a blessing, it increases residents' perceptiveness. A mirror in the foyer draws visitors into the house and a plant obscures an obstructive pillar (see photograph 6). There are a number of ways to apply the human body to the house:

1. Superimpose the body on the house, with the front door area as the head.

2. Use your imagination and intuition when analyzing an odd-shaped house.

3.–4. The most basic way is to impose the ba-gua on the house. Using the ba-gua, feng shui experts can make diagnoses and predictions concerning residents' health and lifespans. If you have a headache, check either the door or the helpful-people position. Obviously, with serious health problems, medical treatment is best, but sometimes feng shui helps.

Accounts of feng shui's effect on the human body abound. For example, in Cincinnati, Ohio, a professor's child had a brain tumor and the medical prognosis was bad. As a last resort, he consulted a feng shui expert who traced the problem to a newly added spiral staircase near their home's entrance, leading from the foyer down to the basement. After installing a vine on the stairwell and solving the helpful people-door position the child recovered and is today a healthy adult.

Chu-shr cures can be applied to various areas of the home to help

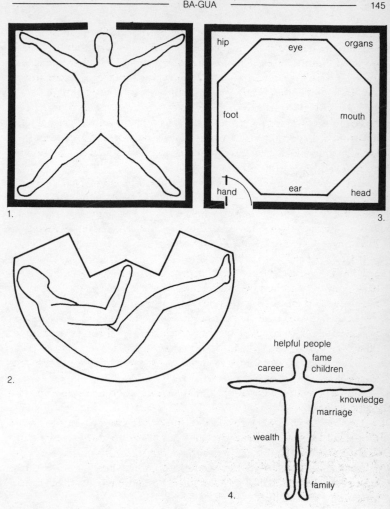

BA-GUA AND THE HUMAN BODY

cure health problems in corresponding parts of the body. A woman undergoing surgery for a torn retina added a mirror at eye level to a window in her bedroom to insure a successful eye operation. She reported the operation was so successful that her vision now is better than it was twenty years ago. Generally, the Nine Basic Cures can be used.

APPENDICES

APPENDIX

While feng shui helps to choose the best places to live, it also addresses how we can position ourselves to thrive, enjoy ourselves, and excel in our vast universe: how we can improve and balance our ch'i. It begins with the physical manipulation of our external surroundings (sying) to create harmony. Taking it one step further, we learn to mirror within ourselves the balance, beauty, and power of the natural world without. These appendices focus on the aspects beyond physical feng shui that can enhance our surroundings and reinforce and improve our ch'i. These are *yi,* or mystical cures for our environment; human ch'i cultivation and meditations; and divination, a sampling of related mystical practices to help bring greater balance and understanding to our lives (astrology, palmistry, dream analysis, Black Hat sect *I Ching,* selected cures).

Appendix 1

YI

Yi is an integral but intangible part of feng shui. It is the realm of the mind and the senses that goes beyond our reactions to our immediate environment. While sying cures are used to literally manipulate surroundings to improve ch'i and residents' luck, yi cures provide a spiritual transformation of negative energy to positive, within a home or in an office or a person.

According to the Black Hat sect of feng shui, yi is the invitation to positive natural forces to enter the home or business. It is both the intention of the individual feng shui expert—a sort of blessing—and/or a permission subconsciously received by the occupant from feng shui or a feng shui adept to succeed, to transcend problems, neuroses, and limitations, and to live a positive, happy, and healthy life.

Yi is a form of faith-healing—the power of the will to believe.

Yi operates in a number of ways, among which are the following:

- Three Secrets
- Ba-gua (see chapter 8)
- Tracing Nine Stars
- Eight-Door Wheel
- Yu nei (adjusting interior house ch'i)
- Yu wai (adjusting exterior house ch'i)
- Constantly Turning Dharma Wheel
- House history
- Others (see Appendices 2 and 3)

Yi is both a subtle suffusing of balance and energy and a psychic manipulation of the atmosphere or spirit of a place. It offers many other ways to change the energy of a place. For example, it can be used to reinforce the cures of sying; yi offers various methods of thinking positively when making an alteration. When a place cannot be physically altered, yi can be invoked to adjust and resolve design problems in a metaphysical way—in using the ba-gua to balance an awkward shape—or in an external way, perhaps to adjust house ch'i to fend off malign effects of a new construction that cuts off a view.

Yi can also improve the ch'i circulation of most places, ranging from the best and the brightest of spaces to the dingiest and most depressing, making them much more livable. For example, an expert might use yu nei (adjusting interior house ch'i) to enliven a dark and dank basement apartment. Or, if a house has been robbed or has had a recent death, employing yi ("sealing the door," the Eight-Door Wheel, or Tracing the Nine Stars) may exorcise malingering anguish.

Yi is possibly the most powerful aspect of Lin Yun's feng shui. Many years of practice and meditation are necessary to master yi, and reading about the transcendental, magical chu-shr cures is not enough. Mystical information must be transmitted orally after the feng shui expert has been given a red envelope with money in it. Hence, much of the yi conveyed here lacks the vital activating ingredient of oral transmission.

THREE SECRETS REINFORCEMENT

This is a ritual way of adding extra strength to any cure. The Three Secrets involves an active blessing that combines three mystical ingredients: body, speech, and mind.

1. *Body:* These are ritual gestures (mudra)—mostly using a hand or hands in poses often seen in pictures of the Buddha—to express intentions or feelings. In everyday life, a mother might raise her hand to warn or scold her child. We shake hands to express friendship. These are common examples of expressive body language. A mudra is a silent invocation by the body. The Blessing Mudra is used for blessings, offerings, and paying the highest homage. The Heart Mudra calms the mind and heart. Men traditionally use their left and women their right hands; for highest results, use the reverse. The Exorcism Mudra is used to dispel malign spirits and to expand ch'i.

2. *Speech:* These are chants conducted initially to recite mantras that have a beneficent influence. For example:

The Six True Words: Om ma ni pad me hum.

The Heart Sutra: Gatay, Gatay, Boro gatay, Boro sun gatay Bodhi So po he.

3. *Mind:* More important than body and speech are our conscious intentions, which are expressed in our thoughts. These can range from a wish or a prayer to a powerful visualization to help either the self or others. For example, if a man is ill, he might visualize a movielike scenario of his recovery process from sickness to healing to finally getting well.

BA-GUA

The many symbolic uses of the propitious octagon of the *I Ching* are explained in chapter 8.

TRACING THE NINE STARS

This is one of the many mystical methods of adjusting and activating ch'i and ridding the home of bad luck. It is tied into the ba-gua, and follows the eight trigrams in a particular sequence. Its purpose is to purify the house of ill fortune and transform it into positive energy. The following is a guideline for what is best carried out by a trained feng shui expert.

The Heart Sutra, a calming meditation, must be performed first.

After entering, locate *jen*—the family position. Direct your ch'i and the house's ch'i from *jen* to *hsun* (wealth) to center to *chyan* (helpful people) to *dwei* (children) to *gen* (knowledge) to *li* (fame) to *kan* (career) to kuen (marriage).

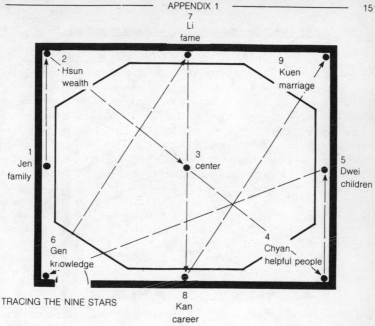

TRACING THE NINE STARS

Trace the Nine Stars through the entire house, penetrating the walls to the garden. Instead of sending your ch'i around, you can walk the path. There are three ways to perform this:

- Walk through the house, touching the Nine Stars in sequence.
- Talk about the nine points, asking the owner questions about each area, drawing the person's ch'i and attention through the nine points starting at *jen*.
- Think of the ba-gua and project your ch'i from point to point, sending blessings to all corners of the house and garden.

THE EIGHT-DOOR WHEEL

Another way to adjust ch'i is with the Eight-Door Wheel. This is a sort of compass with eight life situations that constantly revolve in a sequence: life; injury; imagination; scenery; death; shock; possibility; rest. Of these situations, naturally "life" is the most and "death" the least auspicious. "Rest" and "imagination" are transitional; rest means bad will rise out of good, and imagination is the turning point of bad to good.

Imagine two octagons, one stationary and one (the Eight-Door Wheel) moving. When you enter a house, the Eight-Door Wheel is spinning on the

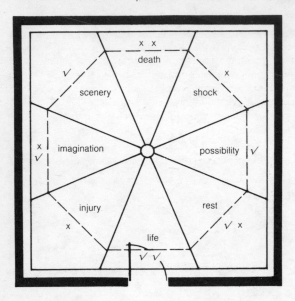

EIGHT-DOOR WHEEL

floor. As you take the first step into the house or apartment, seek to find the gate of "life" and hope it is at the entrance. At the same time, gauge your initial impression, formed by intuition and chance, to indicate what situation you actually stepped on. If you step on one of the seven other doors, identify where "life" is, then visualize rotating the wheel so that "life" moves to the entrance. (Beginners can walk over to "life," then bring it to the front door.) Then visualize gathering the seven other situations and pulling them to "life," and walk to each position to deposit the essence of "life," following the Nine-Star Path. Alternatively, you can pull the trigrams of the stationary ba-gua through "life" in the Nine Star sequence starting at Jen. This can be applied to a house, a room, or a yard (as with the ba-gua).

YU NEI (INTERIOR BLESSING)

Yu Nei is another way to adjust ch'i and resolve an unbalanced shape. Divide the room or building into rectangles. Connect each corner to the center points of the opposite lines. Connect the opposite corners. There will be a crisscross pattern of lines and an inner space formed by these lines bisecting each other—even the space outside the house. Within the inner space, place a living plant or wind chime.

YU WAI (EXTERIOR BLESSING)

Yu wai is a ritual process to encourage new growth. Hold rice in your palm and bless it with the Three Secrets. Sprinkle it around the inner perimeter of the house, then sprinkle the outer shell of the house—or the whole apartment building. The rice symbolizes seeds for new growth of happiness, luck, and prosperity. This is also a sort of exorcism to send away bad ch'i and spirits—appeasing hungry ghosts so they leave in gratitude.

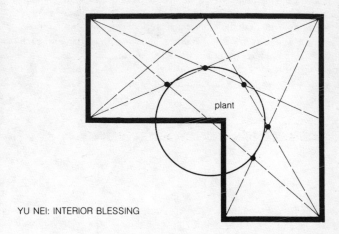

plant

YU NEI: INTERIOR BLESSING

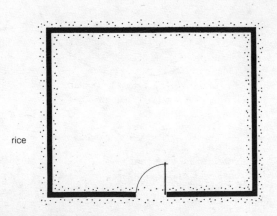

rice

YU WAI: EXTERIOR BLESSING

CONSTANTLY TURNING DHARMA WHEEL

The Constantly Turning Dharma Wheel is a blessing in the form of a meditational juggling act.

Enter the house, look around briefly, then leave and perform the Heart Sutra.

Reenter the house, bringing with you blessings—wishing good things for residents—and Buddha power to add strength to the blessing of the house.

Visualize a wheel spinning in front of you. This is the Dharma Wheel, which encompasses internal sight, sound, and thought. It consists of the Six True Words embodied in six balls of distinct colors, all revolving counterclockwise. Each ball is a universe in itself encircled with six colors, and each of these colors is surrounded by six colors, ad infinitum.

Take the wheel into every part of the house to cleanse and bless the ch'i with your own power and that of the Buddha.

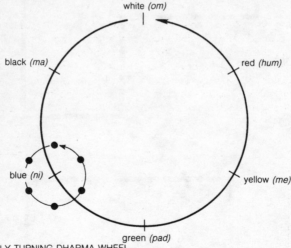

CONSTANTLY TURNING DHARMA WHEEL.

HOUSE HISTORY

The Chinese consider moving into a house to be like stepping into its former owner's shoes and undertaking a similar course of destiny; they believe one adopts the prior owner's habits and repeats his fortune and misfortune within two or three years. For this reason it is always a wise idea to check out the prior owner's situation. Ideally, you want a house or an office where the previous owner prospered and was happy and ended up, through good fortune, moving to even better accommodations. Many Western real-estate agents comment on Chinese clients' curiosity about the seller's life and the house's history. To be safe, the Chinese usually avoid very old homes. Consider whether the former tenant

- died or suffered injury
- moved into a smaller house
- enjoyed social advancement and professional promotions
- was divorced
- underwent bankruptcy, demotion, or job loss.

When a young New York architect moved into the office of a partner who had failed, he asked for feng shui help to avoid a similar fate.

Also, if a house is a bargain, the Chinese suggest looking into its history; something horrible might account for the low price.

SEALING THE DOOR

If you have already bought an ill-fortuned place, Black Hat sect feng shui has a mystical cure called "sealing the door": Place one teaspoon of ju-sha (cinnabar) in a bowl, add drops of strong liquor totaling your age plus one, mix with your middle finger. Dot the inside of the bedroom door, house entrance, side and back doors, even the garage door, and then reinforce with the Three Secrets. Flick the remaining mixture around the centers of rooms and reinforce with the Three Secrets. This cure also can be used to avoid robberies.

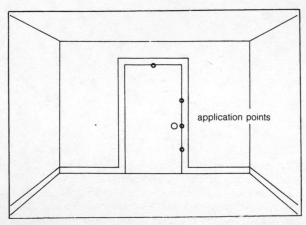

application points

"SEALING THE DOOR "

HOUSEWARMING

Whether a house has bad or good luck, the new occupant is advised to perform a mystical form of housewarming to establish ownership:

Place nine skins of oranges, lemons, or limes in a bowl. Fill the bowl with water and flick the citrus water all around—with wall-to-wall carpeting, use an atomizer—cleansing the place of bad ch'i and bad luck. On moving in, buy a new bed and sheets to get a fresh start.

With businesses, consecration is also important. The Hong Kong and Shanghai Bank always stages lion dances when opening a branch—even at the World Trade Center in New York.

Pig Heaven, a Chinese restaurant in New York, gained immediate popularity after it was consecrated. Carrying a vase with a red ribbon tied around it, and a flute also tied with a red ribbon, the owners followed the feng shui expert around. First the expert mixed nine drops of Bacardi rum with ju-sha and, while chanting, dotted the flute and vase. Next he took a bowl of uncooked rice and scattered it around in all corners of the restaurant and kitchen—even in the woks—all the while maintaining a mudra and chanting.

Appendix 2

CH'I CULTIVATION

This section deals with personal ch'i—how it flows in our bodies and determines our personalities, destinies, actions, and interactions with others, and what we can do to balance and cultivate our ch'i (see chapter 2).

HUMAN CH'I

1. Ideal ch'i circulates smoothly throughout, filling the entire body. It is balanced. It flows up to the top of the head, creating an aura similar to that of Christ or the topknot of the Buddha.

2. Here, ch'i is choked at the throat. Such people tend to be taciturn and reserved. They can't express themselves. Even though they may have a lot to say and want to speak, they are inhibited. They are likely to arrive early to a party, say nothing, and reluctantly leave after everyone has gone home.

3. People like this are compulsive talkers whose ch'i activates their lips and tongues, but doesn't pass the brain. Thus their mouths are overactive. They fire out ch'i like a machine gun, talking without thinking. They may have good intentions, but say too much without sensitivity to others' feelings. Their ch'i makes them not only unable to suppress the urge to talk, but also makes their movements overly gregarious and animated.

4. This is the ch'i of a daydreamer or someone absentminded, whose ch'i is off somewhere else. "The body is there, but not the mind" goes an old Chinese saying.

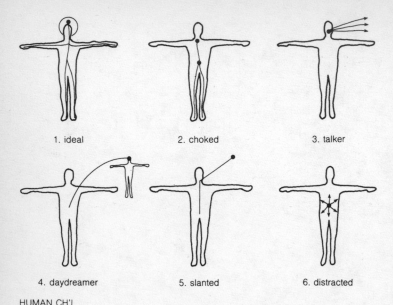

1. ideal 2. choked 3. talker

4. daydreamer 5. slanted 6. distracted

HUMAN CH'I

5. This sort of person is untrustworthy, with oblique intentions. His ch'i is misguided and he is neither straight-thinking nor straight-talking.

6. Though well-intentioned, with many ideas, this person is never contented with what he is doing. He may want to be a lawyer, doctor, or reporter, but will never bother to become one. He is indecisive and distracted; as a result, this person will never develop a strong career.

7. Here the ch'i flows downward, pulling both energy and spirits down. Because ch'i is ready to leave the body, this person will sigh a lot. He will be depressed, self-destructive to the point of being suicidal. Be careful of this kind of person, or you'll have business or emotional problems on your hands.

8. This person is an introvert who thinks too much. The ch'i is concentrated in the head, making him suspicious and withdrawn—pre–nervous breakdown. This ch'i may bring not only mental problems such as paranoia, but also physical symptoms of stress such as ulcers.

9. People like this have a misplaced high self-image, but reality doesn't support it. They are self-deluded and self-defeating.

10. This person is snippy, possessing "porcupine ch'i," a tendency to cut others down, quick with insults and unpleasant comments, and likely to shove in crowds.

11. This person's ch'i is similar to a rigid stalk of bamboo. He is set in his ways and not receptive; the ch'i doesn't reach the ears.

12. This person is moody, unpredictable, and unstable—perhaps a bit schizophrenic—suddenly hot, then just as suddenly cold. You can never tell whether you're on his good or bad side.

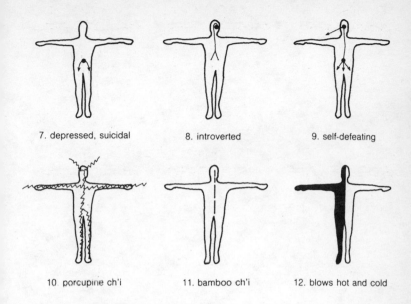

7. depressed, suicidal   8. introverted   9. self-defeating

10. porcupine ch'i   11. bamboo ch'i   12. blows hot and cold

FIVE ELEMENTS AND CH'I

A person's ch'i also contains varying quantities of each element.* Tibetan Tantric Buddhism divides the five elements into 360 degrees, each element comprising 72 degrees—a fifth of a circle. Except for the water element, the ideal is to have a 36-degree "middle road" amount of each element.

Metal. Metal or gold stands for righteousness. A person with little metal is timid, quiet, and cautious. This person doesn't speak out and can't express himself. A person with medium metal talks the right amount; his comments are well thought out. He is a fair person and a patient listener. Possessing a large amount of metal makes a person a brassy and a compulsive talker. He is very argumentative and self-righteous, but doesn't think before talking, and therefore, makes mistakes.

Wood. The element stands for steadfastness and benevolence. A person possessing little wood is like a leaf floating on a pond, being blown this way and that by changes in the wind. He lacks a strong point of view and is too easily influenced by others. A medium wood person is like a healthy young

*Traditional feng shui says women possess only four elements and are always missing one. It takes your dominant element—according to your birthday—and aligns you with a direction. People with strong fire may be advised to have their bed, desk, or entrance face south.

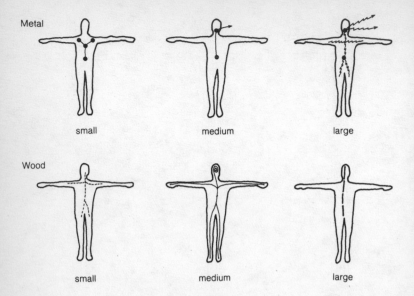

Metal
small   medium   large

Wood
small   medium   large

tree. When the wind blows, its leaves and branches bend, but return to their correct position. This person is flexible and receptive to new ideas, and will incorporate them into his own. A person with lots of wood is like a sturdy palm tree and is impervious to subtle winds, but is so brittle that he may be blown over by a big wind. This person may have lots of ideas, but is stubborn and prejudiced and won't listen to others.

Water. The Chinese divide water into two phases: still and moving. Moving water represents a range of business and social contacts and activities as well as personal drive, mobility, and effectiveness. A person with a slow trickle of water will always stay at home and not go out. His feet won't move much and his mind will not have many thoughts. A frenetic housewife may be like a waterfall, creating a lot of activity during the day; she appears to be going places, but ends up in the kitchen cooking for guests. Similarly, a fountain doesn't travel far. This person is very active, but ends up doing the same things over and over again. A streamlike person has more contact with the outside world, but gets diverted from his course by obstacles. A river is more forceful and gets places faster—sometimes uprooting others in its course. The ocean has unlimited contacts and opportunities—is never at home and is sometimes spread a bit too thin.

Still water reflects insight and intelligence. A dry well is thoughtless, narrow-minded—has tunnel vision. This person's ch'i does not circulate in the head, so his thoughts are often wrong. A ditch has an unbalanced view; when it rains, dirty water drains into the ditch, sullying its clarity. A pond is small but clear, reflecting smartness but limited interests. A reservoir is

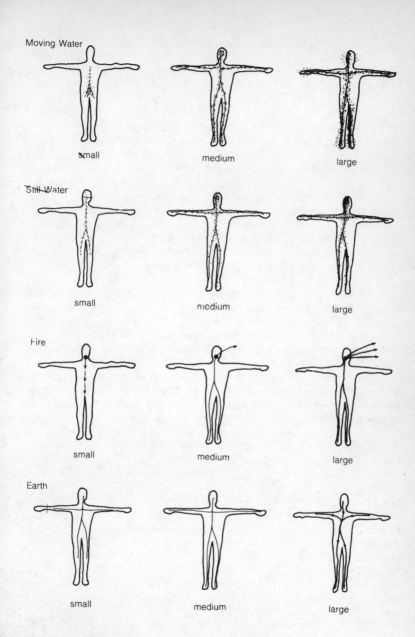

Moving Water

small   medium   large

Still Water

small   medium   large

Fire

small   medium   large

Earth

small   medium   large

clear and large—still enough to reflect the moon—a highly intelligent, lucid, and reflective person.

Fire. Fire is the element of reason, expressiveness, and etiquette. Those with little fire internalize their feelings, swallowing their anger instead of defending themselves. They tend to be unmotivated. They are unexpressive and overly tolerant. Their internalization creates stress on organs. So they suffer from potentially dangerous health problems, especially in the stomach area.

Those with medium fire are considerate and have a strong sense of justice and are capable of criticizing wrongs. Yet they know when to stop.

Those possessing a large quantity of fire are verbally aggressive, loud, and bossy. They assume the role of judge and arbiter, but lack perspective and restraint, so their criticism seems all-inclusive. Because they are intolerant, they tend to be angry, complaining, and never content.

Earth. Earth represents honesty and loyalty. People with a small amount of earth take too good care of themselves and don't share with others. They tend to be insincere, opportunistic, and selfish. Those with a medium amount of earth are reliable, sincere, and faithful. They will consider both themselves and their friends. When dining out, they might suggest going dutch.

Those with a large amount of earth tend to be too earnest and self-sacrificing. They also tend to procrastinate. They are overly generous, to the point of offering money that they can ill afford to give. Their ch'i flows downward a bit.

ADJUSTING THE FIVE ELEMENTS

CURES. Each solution is to be reinforced with the Three Secrets.

Metal. Put a nonmetallic—jade, coral, lapis—ring under the mattress for three or nine days, then wear on the finger representing your age (see Appendix 4).

Wood. Place three potted plants in the house: one near the entrance, one near the living room, and one in the bedroom. If a plant dies, replace it with a healthier and more expensive one.

Water. For still water, place a small round mirror under the mattress in the place where the pillow or your head rests. The first thing every morning, wipe the mirror and visualize clearer thought and a calmer mind. Put it back under the mattress. Repeat for twenty-seven days. For moving water, every day either meet with two new people, write at least two letters, or make phone calls to two friends you haven't seen in six months. Do not include any requests or complaints. Do this for twenty-seven days.

Fire. Every morning, take a deep breath, then exhale with eight small breaths. The ninth breath should be long. Do this nine times for twenty-seven days.

Earth. Drop nine small stones into a small inkpot or vase. Add 70 percent clear water. Expose to the sky. Then put on a home or office desk. Repeat for twenty-six more days, changing water every morning and then exposing it to the sky.

MEDITATION

For many centuries the Chinese have used meditation in conjunction with feng shui to enhance their ch'i, and thus improve their health and future. Feng shui experts meditate before examining a place. Here are two meditations:

The Great Sunshine Buddha Method is used to purify and heal the body and spirit.

1. With palms and arms lifted in the air, turn the head up to face the sun. Imagine the sun embodying *hum,* a sacred sound, swirling down, getting hot, and quickly entering through the third eye. It rushes quickly through the body, filling it and bathing it with heat and sound. When it arrives at the feet, it exits there. Relax arms.

2. Raise arms and palms again. The sun and sound enters through each palm and the third eye. It rushes to the feet, then quickly rebounds to the head and exits there. Relax arms.

3. With arms and palms up, sun and sound reenters the body through the three points and rushes down to the feet. Then it slowly rises, swirling and circling around vital organs and joints and problem spots. Use the sound and bright sunlight to cure such problems, pushing bad ch'i upward and outward. Lower arms and repeat nine times for nine or twenty-seven days. One cycle can be done in the morning, seven others during the day, and the last cycle at bedtime.

The Heart Sutra is a way to activate and improve ch'i. There are several ways to meditate, and many different positions: sitting (or lotus), standing, kneeling—each is fine.

Here is one version: Chant the Heart Sutra (see Appendix 1, Three Secrets speech) to calm your mind. While standing, press palms together as if praying. Visualize a Buddha image—or any deity will do—that comes down and sits on the top of your head. It then enters your body through the top of the skull. It expands to fill your entire body. Filled with the Buddha's ch'i, you become one entity with the Buddha. Next, visualize a fire descending from the sky and entering the top of your head, setting your hair afire. The fire burns progressively down the body, lighting the eyes, nose, ears, mouth, and consciousness. The old self is sloughed away, leaving your body an empty shell occupied by the Buddha. Visualize two pink lotuses, one beneath each foot. Imagine them spawning new pink growth from the bottom of the feet, growing upward, creating a rebirth of a new, purified body, mind, and self. Again, you and the Buddha are one entity. Visualize yourself possessing the Buddha's wisdom, compassion, color, power, and ability. Then picture on your heart a pink lotus flower with two wheels of light on top of it (one red and one white). The red light is stationary while the white wheel spins and embodies *hum,* a sacred sound. It is bright and warm, similar to a ray of sunlight. The white light spins and fills your entire body and then emanates out of your body in all directions, filling the whole universe. There is no limit to how far your light can reach. It shines on the bodies of a pantheon of Buddhas. These Buddhas become bright, and they reflect their light back to you. You receive the light from the pantheon. *(You can stop here and recite the Heart Sutra nine times, or go on to the next steps.)*

When the collective Buddhas' light enters your body, visualize yourself blessing all sentient beings to remove whatever pain, unhappiness, or bitterness is oppressing their hearts. In their resulting happiness, imagine them shining the light back to you. Then, send the light to bless a close friend or family member who might be sick or unhappy. Visualize yourself projecting the Buddha's light on the individual and thus easing his pain, changing his mood from depression to happiness or his health from sickness to recovery. Then the individual will shine the light back to your body.

REINCARNATION

After we die, our ch'i becomes ling again. This ling lingers on earth, traveling to places where we have been when we were alive—perhaps to the hospital, the cemetery, the mortuary, or even our home. There are a number of scenarios for ling. It could be reincarnated and become a human or an animal. Strong ling will avoid reincarnation and not return to human life and ultimately attain nirvana, a state of ultimate bliss. Weaker ling might remain ling on earth. This is a ghost or spirit. If you hear a noise in a very old house, it might come from the ling of a person who died four to five hundred years ago.

Some reincarnations are motivated by ling, who subconsciously want to return to the world and either do good deeds or complete unfinished work. But, after entering the embryo, the ling-ch'i will discover constraints—the baby's body and mind cannot do what the ling intended. After the person matures, the constraints may be overcome and the task can be completed as planned.

Appendix 3

DIVINATION

Feng shui incorporates various forms of divination. Each feng shui discipline offers different techniques of determining auspicious dates, interpreting dreams, and reading futures. Here are some Black Hat sect methods:

ASTROLOGY

Besides there being a right place for the Chinese, there is also a right time: Astrology is an adjunct to all feng shui practices. Many Chinese will not open an office, get married, embark on a trip, or even close a deal until they have consulted a fortune-teller, feng shui expert, or almanac to locate the most propitious date. It is said that Sotheby's in Hong Kong opens shows on specially picked days. Unlike Western astrology, which is month-oriented, a person's year of birth is the determining factor in choosing the correct time for the Chinese. The Chinese use twelve animals to express zodiacal time. Indeed, Chinese time is centered around the number twelve—a twelve-year cycle, twelve phases in a day (two hours each), and twelve months in a year. They say that knowing your Chinese zodiac is essential for choosing worthy partners, spouses, and good times. Astrology also can affect feng shui and the ba-gua; certain house shapes can hurt people born in certain years. A home missing a section in the marriage portion may also be bad for persons born in the years of the ox and the tiger.

THE TWELVE ANIMALS OF THE CHINESE ZODIAC

The Rat (1900, 1912, 1924, 1936, 1948, 1960, 1972, 1984) possesses attributes ranging from charming and humorous to honest and meticulous. The Chinese say those born in these years make good and wise advisers, yet they can never decide for themselves, and change directions constantly. However, rats at times hunger for power and money, leading some to be gamblers, others to be manipulative or petty. Their greed can lead them into a destructive trap.

The Ox (1901, 1913, 1925, 1937, 1949, 1961, 1973, 1985) works hard, patiently, and methodically. These people enjoy helping others. Behind this tenacious, laboring, and self-sacrificing exterior lies an active mind. Although their balance and strength inspire confidence, oxen can seem rigid, stubborn, and slow. They must labor long hours to accomplish little. The Chinese say the time of year and day an ox is born is important in determining life-style. One woman in Hong Kong bragged that she would always be financially provided for, with minimal effort on her part, because she was born on a winter night. Oxen have little to do during the winter months, she explained, because the sweat of summer and fall harvesting is over and it is up to the farmer to feed and keep the oxen warm so they'll have strength for spring planting. Oxen born during agricultural months, however, are sentenced to a life of hard labor.

The Tiger (1902, 1914, 1926, 1938, 1950, 1962, 1974, 1986) is courageous, active, and self-assured, and makes an excellent leader and protector; tigers attract followers and admirers. However liberal-minded tigers may be, they are passionate, rash, and resistant to the authority of others. The Chinese say tigers born at night are particularly restless, for night is the time they hunt. The Western term for a particularly fierce woman is "dragon lady," but the Chinese call her an "old tiger lady." And for this reason some Chinese avoid having children in the Tiger year, for fear of having a daughter.

The Rabbit (1903, 1915, 1927, 1939, 1951, 1963, 1975, 1987) is quick, clever, and ambitious, but seldom finishes what it starts. The rabbit is a social creature, tactful, cool, and sensitive to others. Yet this calm can become aloofness; the sensitivity can be quirky and thin-skinned; and the intelligence can become dilettantish. The rabbit is lucky; with brains and only a little hard labor, it can go far.

The Dragon (1904, 1916, 1928, 1940, 1952, 1964, 1976, 1988) is born in the most desirable year. The imperial family adopted the all-powerful dragon symbol as its royal insignia. Possessing magical powers, the versatile dragon is capable of soaring to the highest heavenly heights or diving to the depths of the sea. On the one hand shrewd, healthy, and full of vitality, the dragon also possesses a mystical side—intuitive, artistic, and strangely lucky. Dragons, however, can plunge pretty low, becoming irritable, stubborn, and impetuous. The dragon's mystical allure may become a bit too otherworldly, making him difficult to get close to. The dragon's unsatisfactory love life leads to a string of loves and marriages.

The Snake (1905, 1917, 1929, 1941, 1953, 1965, 1977, 1989) in Asia prefers to call himself "little dragon," indicating that this, too, is a lucky year. Snakes are wise, philosophical, calm, and understanding. They are receptive and physically alluring, often fickle. Success and fame come easily to snakes. If crossed, they spit venom and can be selfish. They can be lazy and self-indulgent. Their innate elegance can at times be ostentatious.

The Horse (1906, 1918, 1930, 1942, 1954, 1966, 1978, 1990), charming and cheerful, is an extremely likable character. Hard-working, self-possessed, and sharp, the horse skillfully acquires power, wealth, and respect. However, the horse's sometimes appreciated frankness can be tactless. The horse's impatient pursuit of success may become selfish and predatory. Horses can be obstinate.

The Ram (1907, 1919, 1931, 1943, 1955, 1967, 1979, 1991), endowed with innate intelligence and artistic talent, will fare well in business. These people are good-natured and altruistic. However, their successes are limited to money; in family matters they will flounder. They can be a bit too wishy-washy, undisciplined, and irresponsible, and at times show a morose, misanthropic side.

The Monkey (1908, 1920, 1932, 1944, 1956, 1968, 1980, 1992) is lively, likable, and witty. Inventive and intelligent, those born in these years can solve most problems quickly and skillfully and are able to accomplish much in business. Often, however, monkeys are too clever for their own good and can be meddlesome, opportunistic, and unscrupulous to the point of being tricky and manipulative. They tend to be lazy, concentrating on small matters while ignoring more important issues.

The Cock (1909, 1921, 1933, 1945, 1957, 1969, 1981, 1993), hard-working, resourceful, and talented, is a self-assured person. Unlike our Western stereotype of chickens, the Chinese cock is courageous. In groups, they are vivacious, amusing, and popular. But cocks can be a bit too cocksure—strutting their stuff brazenly can be particularly annoying to relatives and close friends.

The Dog (1910, 1922, 1934, 1946, 1958, 1970, 1982, 1994) makes a faithful, honest, and courageous friend, has a deep sense of justice, and inspires confidence. These people tend to be both magnanimous and prosperous, yet they can also be dogged, guarded, and defensive. They accomplish goals quickly. But the dog never really relaxes. Despite appearing calm and at rest, his heart and mind are always jumping.

The Pig (1911, 1923, 1935, 1947, 1959, 1971, 1983, 1995) is sensitive, caring, and indulgent. Not only intelligent and cultured, the pigs also have a streak of bawdiness and earthiness. Their various indulgences can verge on gluttony. Unlike the conniving Machiavellian pigs of *Animal Farm,* Chinese pigs tend to be helpless and insecure. During fat spells they suddenly lose all and are unable to defend themselves, much less attack others. Pigs in general are lucky but lazy.

Traditionally, Chinese matchmakers considered birthdates to determine whether a young man and woman were compatible. Here are some simple charts indicating suitable and incompatible matches (see diagrams).

In picking a lucky year, month, or time of the day, experts use the same configurations as in choosing a compatible spouse. (For days, a complicated Chinese almanac is consulted.) For example, if a person born in the Year of the Monkey wanted to build or bid on a house, buy stock, travel, or enter a lottery, he might do it at 3:00–5:00 P.M., 9:00–11:00 P.M., or 11:00 P.M.–1:00 A.M.

Similarly, house shapes can be related to the twelve animals and time periods. If a corner is missing in the area of the ox, this could be especially bad for those born in the Year of the Ox, the Tiger, the Cock, and the Snake.

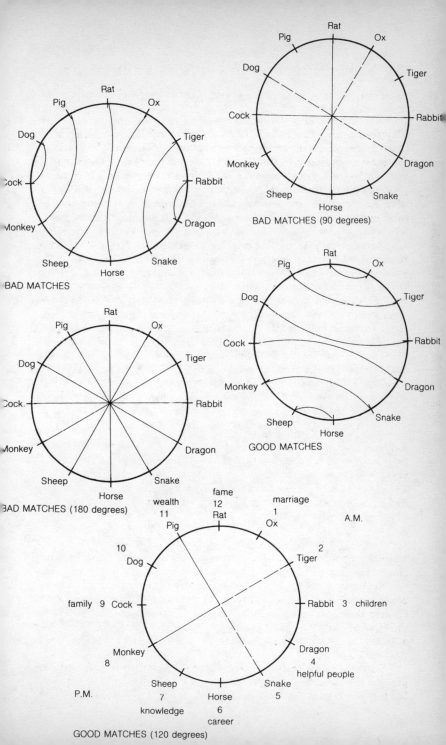

BAD MATCHES

BAD MATCHES (90 degrees)

BAD MATCHES (180 degrees)

GOOD MATCHES

GOOD MATCHES (120 degrees)

PALMISTRY

Our entire bodies show signs reflecting our past, present, and future. One former resident of Shanghai told of reading a young, third-rate actress's palm in the 1930s. It strangely had the markings of a queen or empress. And indeed, this ingenue eventually became Mao Tse-tung's wife, Chiang Ch'ing.

There are lines and facets that the Chinese feel reveal our life's course. If we learn how to read them, we will know what to expect and, through our own efforts, improve our destiny—so the Chinese read faces, palms, ears, and bodies. One Taiwanese face reader predicted that President Kennedy would die in his early forties because his eyes bulged. (Marks or scars above the nose and between the eyes also indicate death, accident, or illness at age forty.) One successful restaurateur with unfortunate marks claims he perplexes face readers because his own visage indicates he should have died ten years ago; he, however, had feng shui help.

The Black Hat sect offers its own form of palmistry, which incorporates traditional methods with the five elements and even the ba-gua.

According to Black Hat sect practice, both the left and right hands offer insight into our destinies. (Traditional palmistry looks at the left hand for the male and the right hand for the female.) A man's left hand is prenatal—what is determined before birth. His right palm shows both the present and how post-birth influences and personality development helped to form his life and altered his prenatal course. For example, good hard work or stubbornness can change our destinies for good or ill.

With women, the left hand is post-birth and the right is prenatal.

Read the prenatal hand first.

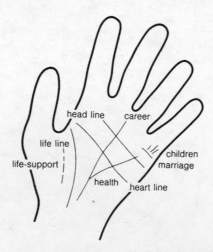

THE PALM
TELL-TALE LINES

LINES

The heart line should be read from side to center. If the heart line is solid and strong, the emotions will be stable. If it branches out, there will be a lot of romances.

A solid and long life line indicates longevity, good health, and safe life. It should be read from the top (birth) down. A broken line may indicate sickness, operation, or accidents.

In the shadow of the life line is the less distinct life-support line. This line, depending on where it lies, can prevent or lessen the effects of an accident. It also represents help or patronage from others.

The career line runs from bottom up. A break indicates a new profession.

The health line is self-explanatory and branches off of the career line.

FINGERS

Fingers represent friends and relations: The thumb is the parents; the pointer is siblings. The self is represented by the middle finger. Friends and spouse is the ring finger. The pinky represents children.

Fingers also indicate ages in one's life. Making sense of this complicated topography also requires knowledge. A mole or a horizontal line in the midsection of the pointer may indicate problems among siblings or an accident or illness in one's late teens. A gap in the life line around age fifty will foretell problems, but an overlapping, parallel life-support line will indicate you will survive. A break in the career line at the mind line may augur a new profession at age thirty-five or thirty-six.

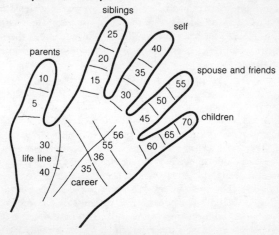

THE PALM AGE, THE SECTIONS OF FINGERS AND THEIR MEANINGS

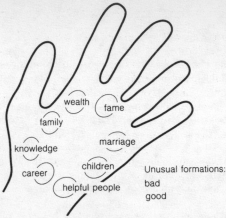

I CHING AND THE PALM

PALM

The Black Hat sect practice applies the *I Ching* to the palm, and interprets our lives from the palm's configurations. For example, bumps are good, flat areas are so-so or normal, and indentations are bad. Lesser lines that crisscross the hand are also read. Vertical lines are good; horizontal lines are bad. A Chinese palmist will inspect a palm for unusual shapes caused by bisecting lines that may bode well or ill for its owner. For example, a triangle in the wealth position may mean financial losses, or a square in the children area may indicate good fortune for offspring.

The Chinese also have various ways of reading the face and ears. One of the methods is to use the ba-gua. Bumps, scars, and beauty marks in one of the eight areas can indicate past or present problems for relatives and friends. Colors or hues under the eyes are associated with events: yellow brings celebration, black brings illness, white foretells the death of a family member, red brings government and legal tangles, and green augers shock and worries.

DREAMS

Dreams—our nighttime subconscious state—are another way to understand and expand knowledge of our ch'i, health, thoughts, and lives.

A person's daytime ch'i differs from his nighttime ch'i. As explained before, our ch'i is affected by many elements: the universe, society, politics, economics, feng shui, our own ch'i, and that of others. Dreams primarily express the effects of our own ch'i and the ch'i of others.

Nighttime ch'i can behave in a number of different ways:

1. When both the physical body and ch'i are tired, you will not dream.

2. When the body is tired, but ch'i is still active and doesn't want to leave the body and let it rest, ch'i may open the eyes or make the body

toss and turn. This will lead to insomnia, heart palpitations, and ultimately a nervous breakdown.

3. If ch'i is weak day and night, the person will have strange dreams at night and will daydream during waking hours. This person tends to be vague and have bad judgment. For example, he may trust a person with bad intentions. This person also will have no energy to develop in a career and will suffer from chronic bad health.

4. When the body is tired and resting, but the ch'i is still lively and active and travels out of the body to sightsee or visit a friend, the ch'i will return and occupy the mind, and when the body wakes, the ch'i will remind the person of its nocturnal travels and activities. This is a dream.

Our dreams are affected by several elements:

1. Our senses, which are influenced by good and bad stimuli
2. Remembrance of good and bad experiences
3. Our desires
4. Our fears
5. Imbalances in our body organs or elements

Thus, the state of each person's ch'i also contributes to the type of dream. People with too much yin dream of water. People with too much yang dream of fire. People with lots of both yin and yang dream of two people arguing, fighting, and killing each other. Those with a small amount of yin and yang dream of being oppressed or killed. Those with upward-moving ch'i will dream they can fly or float in the air or water. People with downward-moving ch'i dream of falling into water or off a cliff.

The physical body affects dreams, too. A person who has eaten too much will dream of donating things to others. A person who goes to bed hungry will dream of taking things. Those with bad livers will be angry in their dreams, while those with lung ailments will dream of crying.

Dreams can be divided into three time spans: a dream in the first part of the night is one influenced by the day's happenings and thoughts; a dream in the second part of the night represents our past experiences or lives; a dream in the third section, right before we wake up, is a premonition.

Dreams also indicate good and bad luck. Dreams of the sun, dragons, or a head are all good signs. Dreams of feet, tails, or a deep hole are bad omens. The worst dreams are of the room or house the sleeper actually is in. This is a sign of the sleeper's energy being oppressed by bad ch'i, so that his own ch'i cannot escape and travel.

A living person who dies in a dream will have very good luck, and so will the dreamer. If a dead person is alive in a dream, this is a good omen for the dreamer.

It is not necessarily bad if you cannot dream. But the Black Hat sect has a cure for nightmares. Within three days of having the dream, write on a round piece of paper: "I had a nightmare and now I write on a high wall. The sun rises and shines and the bad dream becomes good, thus the outcome will be good." Paste the paper outside on a high place or on a bulletin board at night.

I CHING

Some say that the *I Ching* is the oldest Chinese book—or *ching*—dating back nearly five thousand years to the legendary Hsia Dynasty. The term *I* 易 means change: it symbolizes one day, the sun 日 and moon 月 progressing, yet eternally recurring. Some say *I* 蜴 is a chameleon 蜴 that changes colors to protect itself, thus the *I Ching* is interpreted as a handbook to help us adapt to the demands and dangers of society and life. But most likely, while it is all these, the *I* 易 stands for the complementary interaction of yin and yang, the two primordial forces of the universe from which all things spring.

The *I Ching* is the work of several minds. The legendary Fu Hsi, observing nature's continual passage from day into night into day, created the eight trigrams; King Wen, the founder of the Chou Dynasty, combined the trigrams and explained the resulting hexagrams' meanings. His son, the Duke of Chou, provided the meaning of the lines. And, so legend has it, his contemporary, Confucius, wrote the commentaries.

The following is a Black Hat sect ritual to create a positive atmosphere when seeking *I Ching* wisdom. It will help increase one's receptivity to profound and useful advice and insight.

HOW TO USE THE I CHING—BLACK HAT SECT METHOD

1. Take six coins—five of the same size and one either larger or smaller to indicate the "changing" line.

2. Think of a divinity—God, the Buddha, Allah—who will answer your question. Then ask the deity for help and guidance.

3. Ritual before tossing coins:

- Calm down, empty your mind of ideas and worries. Concentrate on what you are doing.
- Recite the Heart Sutra, a mantra for calming the mind, nine times. (see Appendix 1—Three Secrets Speech)
- Look skyward.
- Inhale and exhale nine times.
- Ask a deity for guidance; be specific.

4. Now shake the coins in your palms or a turtle shell nine times. Without looking, pick out a coin at random. This is the bottom line of your hexagram. Heads will be yang—, tails will be yin--. Then, one by one, pick the other coins until you have six lines—a hexagram. Note where the small coin's changing line is.

5. Using a translation of the *I Ching,* read the resulting hexagram from bottom to top. Read the commentary for each line and the hexagram.

Then flip the small coin to change heads (yang) to tails (yin) or vice versa, and read the changed hexagram, paying special attention to the changing line. Here is an example of a hexagram, which represents unity. After reversing the small coin, which represents the changing line, the hexagram would have a new meaning.

5th coin; yang (heads)

1st coin; yin (tails)

SELECTED CURES

The following are personal practices related to feng shui to help improve your ch'i. There are countless cures—sometimes carried out internally, sometimes by altering one's environment. For example, an executive placed a rooster feather in his desk drawer to improve business; a couple placed nine stones in a plant in the wealth position of their house to increase their wealth; a woman hung a crystal ball in the relevant organ position of her home to ensure the success of an operation.

Traditionally, these cures work as a kind of blessing dispensed by a feng shui master only after he is given a red envelope containing money. Though the following cures are not strictly medical, they are ways in which you can change your physical and mental orientation to soothe and assist yourself or others.

BACKACHE CURE

One Black Hat sect cure for backache—when all else fails—is to put nine pieces of chalk in a rice bowl that contains a little uncooked rice. Place the bowl in the spot under the bed directly beneath your back.

ACQUIRING MARRIAGE CH'I

This cure is for people hoping to get married. Those who are already married can also follow this cure, because the ch'i of wedding is among the happiest and best.

Obtain nine objects from a newly married couple, or have them touch nine of your own on their wedding day or within ninety days of the wedding. Have the bride touch each item. Visualize that you acquire marriage ch'i when she hands over the nine objects. Put them in the marriage position of your bedroom.

A PRENUPTIAL RITUAL

One tradition to ensure a solid marriage calls for the bride to bring two cups of water to the car before going to the wedding, and then spill it on the road. After entering the car, she should not look back. The Chinese have a saying: "A daughter who gets married is like spilled water—she cannot return home."

A CONCEPTION RITUAL

The wife takes her husband's lunch or dinner bowl—without rinsing or cleaning it—and puts nine raw lotus seeds and nine dried dates in the dish. She then fills the bowl with water to 70 percent of its capacity and puts it under the bed (directly under her abdomen). Before installing the bowl under the bed, she exposes the bowl to the moon and invites the ling in the atmosphere to enter her house. She reinforces this cure with the Three Secrets. The first thing every morning for nine days, the wife replaces the water with fresh water and exposes the bowl to the sky, inviting inside the ling of the universe. After nine days, she pours the contents into a houseplant and buries the seeds and dates in the soil. She places the pot near the front door and performs the Three Secrets. The instructions above are repeated twice. The second plant is placed in the living room near the entrance door, and the third pot is placed in the bedroom in the children position. Each time, the cure is reinforced with the Three Secrets. Avoid dusting under or moving the bed.

Appendix 4

YUN LIN TEMPLE'S FENG SHUI

Buildings that do not need feng shui improvements are rare. When the Yun Lin Temple was moved into a new house in Berkeley, California, several alterations had to be made. The first consideration was its prior occupants; the sixty-year-old Colonial-style mansion has had only two previous owners, who lived to advanced age, an indication of stable ch'i. Lin Yun explained the other assets and deficiencies of the Temple's new home during a walking tour.

Standing at the entrance gate, he surveyed the simpler houses below and commented that the earth ch'i of the area was concentrated where his house stood. Looking up forty-two stairs to a columned portico, he said the height gave the building an impressive, stately air and commanding views. Four two-story columns served to support the house ch'i. Although the slope was too steep, he planned to shorten the climb with a landscaped terrace adorned with a large stone Buddha. Twin pines on either side of the entrance gate were also attractive and auspicious features, which Lin Yun referred to as "welcoming-guests pines." They served as natural guardians, sheltering the building and protecting and uplifting its spiritual ch'i. (The two trees were also a natural signature for Lin Yun: the name Lin—also the Chinese character for "forest"—is created by using two "tree" characters.) Stepping inside, Lin Yun explained that the stairway was too close to the entrance. He hoped to conceal the stairs by constructing a mirrored wall that would also reflect and draw in the two pines and their auspicious connotations of longevity.

Standing in the foyer, he pointed out that four consecutive doors leading from the front to the back door lined up, funneling ch'i too quickly. This would not only cause physical problems along the central meridian of the bodies of the frequent guests, but would also create a divisive axis down the center of the house that would cause many arguments among the Temple members. This could be remedied by hanging a crystal ball or a wind chime in the foyer to break up the line of the doors. Upstairs, after pointing out a panoramic view of the bay area, he touched a slanted door, saying it could portend disaster, and made a note to resolve the dangerous structure by hanging a crystal ball directly inside the room to which it lead. To top it all off, he planned to install an electric fan in the attic skylight, which would raise the ch'i of the entire house.

Looking around the house, Lin Yun said, "There's much to be done. We'll do it step-by-step, and once the feng shui is complete, it will be a very special place."

The Yun Lin Temple is the first temple of the Black Hat sect of Tibetan Tantric Buddhism to be established in the United States of America. The temple opened its doors in October 1986, and is located at 2959 Russell Street, Berkeley, CA 94705 (telephone: 415-840-2347).